Holy Work with Children

HORIZONS *IN* RELIGIOUS EDUCATION is a book series sponsored by the Religious Education Association: An Association of Professors, Practitioners, and Researchers in Religious Education. It was established to promote new scholarship and exploration in the academic field of Religious Education. The series will include both seasoned educators and newer scholars and practitioners just establishing their academic writing careers.

Books in this series reflect religious and cultural diversity, educational practice, living faith, and the common good of all people. They are chosen on the basis of their contributions to the vitality of religious education around the globe. Writers in this series hold deep commitments to their own faith traditions, yet their work sets forth claims that might also serve other religious communities, strengthen academic insight, and connect the pedagogies of religious education to the best scholarship of numerous cognate fields.

The posture of the Religious Education Association has always been ecumenical and multi-religious, attuned to global contexts, and committed to affecting public life. These values are grounded in the very institutions, congregations, and communities that transmit religious faith. The association draws upon the interdisciplinary richness of religious education connecting theological, spiritual, religious, social science and cultural research and wisdom. Horizons of Religious Education aims to heighten understanding and appreciation of the depth of scholarship resident within the discipline of religious education, as well as the ways it impacts our common life in a fragile world. Without a doubt, we are inspired by the wonder of teaching and the awe that must be taught.

Holy Work with Children

Making Meaning Together

TANYA MARIE EUSTACE CAMPEN

◆PICKWICK *Publications* · Eugene, Oregon

HOLY WORK WITH CHILDREN
Making Meaning Together

Horizons in Religious Education Series

Copyright © 2021 Tanya Marie Eustace Campen. All rights reserved. Except for brief quotations in critical publications or reviews, no part of this book may be reproduced in any manner without prior written permission from the publisher. Write: Permissions, Wipf and Stock Publishers, 199 W. 8th Ave., Suite 3, Eugene, OR 97401.

Pickwick Publications
An Imprint of Wipf and Stock Publishers
199 W. 8th Ave., Suite 3
Eugene, OR 97401

www.wipfandstock.com

PAPERBACK ISBN: 978-1-7252-9620-6
HARDCOVER ISBN: 978-1-7252-9621-3
EBOOK ISBN: 978-1-7252-9622-0

Cataloguing-in-Publication data:

Names: Campen, Tanya Marie Eustace, author.

Title: Holy work with children : making meaning together / by Tanya Marie Eustace Campen.

Description: Eugene, OR: Pickwick Publications, 2021 | Horizons in Religious Education Series | Includes bibliographical references.

Identifiers: ISBN 978-1-7252-9620-6 (paperback) | ISBN 978-1-7252-9621-3 (hardcover) | ISBN 978-1-7252-9622-0 (ebook)

Subjects: LCSH: Children (Christian theology). | Christian education of children. | Church work with children.

Classification: BV639.C4 E 2021 (print) | BV639.C4 (ebook)

Scripture quotations marked NRSV are from New Revised Standard Version Bible, copyright ©1989 National Council of the Churches of Christ in the United States of America. Used by permission. All rights reserved worldwide.

Scripture quotations marked CEB arefrom the Common English Bible®, CEB® Copyright ©2010, 2011 by Common English Bible.™ Used by permission. All rights reserved worldwide.

06/25/21

Dedicated to all the children I journey with.

Thank you for teaching and inspiring me.

CONTENTS

Editorial Review Board | ix
Editors' Preface | xi
Acknowledgments | xiii

Chapter 1: Starting from the Very Beginning: A Story Created out of Wonder and Curiosity | 1
Chapter 2: Children as Theologians: Making Meaning Together | 15
Chapter 3: Holy Conversation: Listening to Children | 28
Chapter 4: Holy Conversations with God | 51
Chapter 5: Tools for this Holy Work | 69
Chapter 6: Faithful Praxis: Partnering with God's Children | 90

Appendix: Research Methodology: Wondering with and Listening to the Children | 109
Bibliography | 113

HORIZONS in RELIGIOUS EDUCATION—EDITORIAL REVIEW BOARD

Editorial Review Board
—Jack L. Seymour (co-editor), Garrett-Evangelical Theological Seminary

—Hosffman Ospino (co-editor), Boston College

—Mai-Anh Le Tran (co-editor), Garrett-Evangelical Theological Seminary

Class of 2021
—Dean G. Blevins, Nazarene Theological Seminary

—N. Lynne Westfield, The Wabash Center for Teaching and Learning in Religion and Theology

—Maureen O'Brien, Duquesne University

Class of 2022
—Elizabeth Conde-Frazier, Association for Hispanic Theological Education

—Sheryl Kujawa-Holbrook, Claremont School of Theology

—Boyung Lee, Iliff School of Theology

EDITORIAL REVIEW BOARD

Class of 2023
—Deborah Court, Bar Ilan University
—Harold Horell, Fordham University
—Katherine Turpin, Iliff School of Theology

EDITORS' PREFACE

We are pleased to announce the seventh book in the Religious Education Association, *HORIZONS in Religious Education* series. Dr. Tanya Marie Eustace Campen, director of Intergenerational Discipleship of the Rio Texas Annual Conference of The United Methodist Church in San Antonio, Texas, focuses on ministries with children. Drawing on both her extensive ministry and face-to-face research with children and their parents, Dr. Campen describes how children are reflective about religious thinking. She shows how they attend to their communities, draw from the religious and cultural wisdom that surrounds them, and question and make decisions about how to respond to experiences of God's presence and calling. She sensitively introduces us to these children, tells their stories, highlights the cultures and communities from which they come, and shows us how they seek to make meaning in their lives.

It is interesting to speculate how this 2020 period in our history will be remembered twenty years from now. Will we look back and see this crisis time as formative for a new future? Will it be a disruptive and transformative moment in religious education when we were able to sustain the religious formation of children and support families in their role as faith educators or will we see it as a blip, an interruption of the normative? And what are we writing now that will provide perspective on these unprecedented times in which we live, and how we help our children both make sense of it and respond with justice, mercy, kindness, and acts of peace?

Literature on children's spirituality is certainly not a new topic in the field of religious education. In 2006, the important collection of articles, *Nurturing Child and Adolescent Spirituality* invited readers to learn from each other's faith tradition so as to be aware of what we share and how

Editors' Preface

we are different.[1] And literature to help congregations and families raise children in faith continues to help us think about the ways we honor and nurture the spiritual lives of our children. Perhaps the literature is so great because the need is so great.

Rev. Dr. Tanya Marie Eustace Campen has written a book that invites the reader to pause and rethink the ways that we help children connect their faith with their lives in the world. Through stories of children she has encountered, she reminds us of that which we already know but sometimes forget: children are theologians, and our ministry with them is holy work.

This book offers theological educators, pastors, congregations, and caregivers the chance to consider both the models we use and the approaches we take in helping our children grow in their ability to think theologically and to experience the way the Holy is present in their lives. It can be mined in seminary and college classes to assist students to build on and shape their ministries to children. Furthermore, it can be used in congregational settings to help adults who talk, live, and engage in acts of justice with children grow more deeply in their own faith and their service with children.

Holy Work with Children: Making Meaning Together shows us how to stand beside and support children as they recognize, claim, and respond to God's presence and love in their lives. Moreover, Dr. Campen offers us tools to attend to the settings where faith formation takes place in our congregations: tools of story, liturgy and ritual, relational awareness, memory markers, wonder, and work. She invites us to join with children in the amazing work of listening to God, drawing on our traditions, and seeking to live in ways that enrich and transform our worlds. We highly recommend this very practical book grounded in in-depth research and drawing on rich educational and theological resources. May we seek to be faithful as we join with children in the dance of meaning making and living justly.

—Jack L Seymour, Professor Emeritus of Religious Education at Garrett-Evangelical Theological Seminary, Evanston, Illinois, USA Co-editor of *HORIZONS*

—Elizabeth Caldwell, Adjunct Faculty, Vanderbilt University Divinity School, Nashville, Tennessee, USA *HORIZONS* Editorial Board

1. Yust et al., *Nurturing Child and Adolescent Spirituality.*

ACKNOWLEDGMENTS

My work in ministry with children began as an adolescent volunteer in my local United Methodist Church's nursery. What began with a love for children grew into a deep respect for their wisdom and the gifts they bring into God's transformative and beatific process.

To the many faith communities, staff, volunteers, and families who have welcomed me into their fold as I grew into my calling and joined me in this important work- Thank you!

Much of this book comes out of my dissertation and doctoral research project. I am grateful to my advisor, Margaret Ann Crain, and dissertation committee, Jack Seymour, Stephen Ray, and Dori Baker—thank you for believing in me, encouraging me, and most of all for teaching me. My thanks also to my mom, Natalie Eustace, and Aunt, Ginny Sidrony, for the time and love you gave to reading and editing all the pages that came before and found their way into this manuscript. To Meredith Hoxie Schol and Erin Simmons, my research assistants—thank you for joining me in the work of paying attention, wondering faithfully, and listening deeply.

Elizabeth Caldwell, Jack Seymour, and Ulrike Guthrie, my editors—thank you for seeing the possibility of this book when I was distracted by the many pieces of the kaleidoscope. With every twist and turn, you were my shepherds, calling me to honor the vision, stories, and details, as we shaped this book into being. Thank you!

Over the years I have been blessed by the presence of strong women who have guided and supported me, showing me the way. Kaci Boylan, Sarah Cannon, Ann Dieterle, and Stacy Kimpel- Thank you for listening to my wonderings and for offering me years of friendship and encouragement. To my colleagues in ministry and conversation partners, Christine Hides and

ACKNOWLEDGMENTS

Kathy Pittenger, thank you for your encouragement and wisdom. To Heath Howe, my guide and compass—words cannot express my gratitude. Thank you for providing the light that showed me the way.

Many thanks to my immediate and extended family, who have been on this journey with me and influenced who I am. I am grateful that God has blessed me with such a wonderful support system and cheerleading section. To my Godchildren—thank you for teaching me, wondering with me, and letting me into your hearts. To Thumper, my beloved son—you came into this world during the writing process and have inspired me to complete this project. You made me a Mama, giving me a new understanding and experience of what it means to journey with, care for, and love another precious person. To my supportive, patient and faithfully present husband, Ryan, thank you for listening to my millions of wonderings, all of the possibilities, and for encouraging me through all of the distractions. I love you all SO BIG!

Finally, I take my hat off to the inspiration for this project and my guides on this journey: the children who participated with me in this research project—thank you for showing me the way. Thank you for trusting me with your stories, experiences, thoughts, wisdom, and insight. I am forever grateful and forever changed.

chapter 1

STARTING FROM THE VERY BEGINNING

A Story Created out of Wonder and Curiosity

> It was a normal Sunday morning. The children's minister at a United Methodist church, I was scurrying around making sure everything was ready for that morning's ministries. As I raced up the stairs to check the copy machine, I saw a family (Mom, Dad, Son) standing in the hallway looking slightly lost. I slowed my pace, walked up to the family and introduced myself. The parents looked at each other, then at their son, and finally at me. The mom took a deep breath and said: "He has a question for you" (motioning to their son). I quickly got down on eye level with the young child and said: "Hi, I'm Tanya, I'm the pastor for children here at this church. I'm so glad you're here. Do you have a question for me?" The child looked down at the ground, shuffled his feet, and asked, "How do I know I believe in God?"

The world seemed to stop for a moment as I considered the serious nature of the boy's question. Recognizing that I did not have a simple answer, nor the only let alone "correct" answer, I took a deep breath, looked into the child's eyes, and said: "That is a big question." I took another deep breath and said: "You know, I wonder about that too." Finally, after gathering my wits for a moment, I responded to his question with another question: "I wonder when you have felt God?"

This young child responded, looking around the building: "Sometimes when I am in a special place." "Me too," I replied. "Sometimes I feel God's presence when I am in worship in the special place we call the Sanctuary. I wonder how else you might know about God?" He responded: "When people tell me about God and I hear stories." I smiled and said, "You know, I also learn about God from other people. When people share their God stories with me, I learn how they experience and know they believe in God. This helps me when I am unsure." The child nodded and looked at me and smiled.

Sensing his mother's growing impatience, I knew our time was up and ended by saying: "I am grateful for other people who help me know God exists." He responded: "Me too." "Thank you for having this important conversation with me," I said.

I had just had a very real theological conversation with a young child. I smiled as I noticed how we had created a space in which we could wonder together about God's presence in our lives. Together we had engaged in a meaning-making process, each of us questioning and discerning our own theological understanding of the Divine. This child left me wondering about my own faith journey, my own experiences, and my own questions. I have pondered his question for many years since that encounter, and continue to ask myself the boy's question: "How do we know we believe in God?" I am not sure either of us left the conversation having the correct or only answer, but for a moment we had created a space where together we could question, experience, wonder, and reflect on God's presence in our lives.

This question continues to guide me as I write in the midst of the global COVID-19 pandemic and as I alongside many others are finding ways to address the deep reality of racism in our communities and nation. I find myself pondering the wisdom I have gained from sitting with and listening to children. In a world that is filled with such division, hurt, and illness, I too wonder: "How do we know we believe in God?" How can children guide us in finding faithful ways to respond to the realities of the world we live in? How do they show us a path towards love, unity, hope, and healing?

Personal experiences help me realize how paying attention and listening to children opens a space for the entire faith community to experience and claim *Emmanuel,* God with us. When I wonder with children, I begin to see and understand God differently, and I hear God's call more clearly. As I engage in this holy work that I describe as ministry *with* children, my experiences lead me to reflect on the theological, scriptural, and developmental impacts of the children's wonderings, stories, and discoveries. In response, I grow in my faith and my understanding of children and their faith formation process. As children continue to guide and teach me, I find myself discovering new and faithful ways to be in ministry with the youngest members of the Body of Christ.

Ministry with children has taught me how to pay attention, listen, wonder, and respond to God's presence in the world. As we look for God's light and love in this world, and as we seek faithful ways to respond, my prayer is that the wisdom of children will provide wisdom and insight for us adults and for those we are in ministry with. This book is a summary of my experiences of engaging in ministry *with* children. In the following pages, I share with you what children have taught me, and I describe how we engage in this holy work together. I hope that you, the reader, will likewise find ways to deepen your theological understanding of children as we find faithful ways to support them in the transformative work God calls them to.

GOD IS WITH US: HOLY CONVERSATION WITH CHILDREN

Faithful ministry with children begins with a deep respect and understanding of God's active presence in the lives of all people, no matter their age. As adults in ministry with children, our work is to create a space for persons of all ages to hear God. When I take the time to sit and listen to children, I discover that God "shows up" in new and exciting ways. Perhaps before this recognition I was not paying attention, distracted by other tasks, or maybe I was not listening closely but instead was mentally rehashing my list of worries or my to-do list. Whatever it was that caused me to miss God's voice, I have learned that the act of setting aside time to listen opens up new possibilities. It gives me space to wonder to what or to whom God is calling me next. When I create space for the youngest members of the body of Christ to do this work, I find that my eyes are opened and my heart hears more clearly what God is calling me to do.

Yet in the end, it is not all about me. No, it is about learning how to do the holy work of faith formation together. Together, we—adults in ministry with children—can wonder with the children in our communities about God's presence in our lives. This hard work of wondering helps us make meaning about God, our relationships, and the world.

As families and communities face the realities of the COVID-19 global pandemic together I have witnessed people of all ages wondering together. Children appearing in digital boxes via zoom share their joys, their concerns, and their hopes too. One young child I met via a virtual camp experience shared that "even though we are all apart, I'm grateful for ways God brings us together!" During this time, I have watched families worship together—dancing and singing on zoom as they experience God in their homes. I have listened deeply to ministry leaders struggling to identify a new path in the midst of the unknown and uncertainty. "Everything is changing, and I do not know where God is calling me next," shared one ministry leader. Another named a deep calling and concern as to how to sit with children and hear their wonderings in response to the racism in our nation as they discern ways to do the hard and holy work of nurturing antiracist children who seek to ensure equality and justice for all. These are big questions and the researcher in me keeps asking: "Have you talked with your children?"

The only way we can begin to address all of the inequality, injustice, and divisiveness is to engage in holy conversation together as we discern how God is calling us to respond and commit to doing that work together. The only way to know how to support one another in the process of faith formation during a global pandemic and beyond is to listen to one another, to pay attention to the reality and needs of our community, and to ask: "God how are you calling us to love you and our neighbors in this day, in this time, in response to these realities?"

By doing this work of faith formation together, we grow in our faith and in our relationships with God and each other. It is a reciprocal growing process. When we create space to listen, we find ways to leave behind the busy and loud voices of the world and listen more carefully to God's still and quiet voice within and to each other. It is through this holy work that all of us as God's children discover our calling together as the Body of Christ and find new ways to love God and neighbor, together.

In these holy moments, the children and faithful adults wonder together how God moves and participates in the life of creation. This can be done through stories. Using the *Godly Play* curriculum, we sit together watching and listening as God's stories unfold.[1] One of the children's favorite stories is the *Parable of the Good Shepherd*. This parable combines Psalm 23 with the Parable of the Good Shepherd found in the Gospel of John. In this *Godly Play* story, sheep are moved across a flat piece of felt. They move through the good grass, the cool, still, fresh water and the places of danger.[2] As the sheep move, the children and I wonder together: "I wonder

---

1. Berryman, *Complete Guide to Godly Play: Volume 1*.
2. Berryman, *Complete Guide to Godly Play*, 3:60.

when you have been to the good grass . . . I wonder when you have felt the cool, fresh water . . . I wonder when you have been in a place of danger?" In response, the children share their life experiences: moments when they lay in the grass on a summer day with their families; times when they smelled the grass as they kicked a soccer ball and made their first goal; stories of summers spent swimming in Lake Michigan and playing in the water with friends. Children share times when they were lost or afraid.

> "One time I got lost in a shopping mall," one seven-year-old boy shared. "I remember looking around and seeing a bunch of people but I couldn't find my mom."
>
> "How did that make you feel?" I asked.
>
> "Really scared," he said. "And alone," he continued.
>
> "What happened next?" I asked.
>
> "A friendly woman found me and asked me if I knew where my mom was. She showed me the booth where I could talk to someone who worked at the mall who could help me."
>
> "I wonder how that made you feel?" I responded.
>
> "Good, but kinda scared—I didn't know if she was a good person."
>
> "How did you find your mom?" I asked.
>
> "The mall person helped me. She called over the intercom and my mom came to me."
>
> "Wow," I said, "I bet that felt good."
>
> Yes," the child answered. "I was so happy and so relieved . . . it was like when the good shepherd found the lost sheep . . . She held my hand tightly as we walked to the car together . . . Just like the Good Shepherd . . . she led me to safety."

In such moments, children help me see the connections between scripture and real life events. This is foundational to the meaning-making process. Our interactions reveal how God moves in and through their wonderings and stories. Children reveal God—or in this boy's case, Christ as the Good Shepherd—at work in their lives. As another child said: "God always protects me when I am scared . . . sometimes at night I pray that God will keep the bad dreams from coming . . . most of the time they stay gone." These holy conversations remind every person in that holy space that God is active in our lives, that if we pay attention we can see and feel God's presence and love. "God is always there. You just have to stop and look."

We are called and formed by our conversations and ministry with children. When I sit with children and listen with them to the biblical stories, or when we wonder about our response to these stories, I always discover something new about myself and my relationship with the Divine.

I believe the children do this holy work too. One afternoon, after a long day of work and school, sixteen children and I sat together in a circle on the floor of a Chicago church classroom. The children listened as I shared the story of the *Holy Family,* another *Godly Play* story and creation of Jerome Berryman. In this story, we saw a wooden figure of baby Jesus with his arms out wide. I said: "Here is the little baby reaching out to give you a hug."[3] Then I sat back to give everyone time to take in this part of the story.

As I sat, I reflected on the small wooden figure. I thought about the Jesus I had studied for so many years in seminary and into my years as an ordained pastor. I thought about Jesus as a baby, and I remembered my Godchildren as infants. I remembered their arms wide open as they cried as if to say: "Somebody please pick me up. Somebody please love me." I thought about what it must have been like for Mary, Jesus' mother, to hold baby Jesus, to feel his warmth, and to worry about his future as she willed him to sleep so that she too could get some rest. As I thought about all of this, I saw the wooden figure of Jesus with new eyes . . . , and I felt comforted. I felt the peace that comes from holding a sleeping infant and the joy that comes when a child reaches out and gives you a hug. I thought about the blessing Christ gives in his eternal grace, presence, and love.

As I pondered such things, I heard a small voice next to me whisper: "Jesus is always there, ready to give us a hug . . ." I waited in case there was more. Then I heard: ". . . I like that," as the child smiled slowly and sat back looking satisfied with her revelation and the truth she had spoken.

When we experience the stories together and when we take the time to wonder and reflect, we experience anew the truth that pours out of the Holy Scriptures, and we find ways to claim this truth as our own. These holy moments affirm children as theologians and support systematic theologian David H. Jensen's claim that the "theological understandings of children matter; they have an impact, for good or for ill, on the way the church and

---

3. Berryman, *Complete Guide to Godly Play,* 2:83.

society nurtures or neglects their unique lives."[4] When we create space for children to do this holy work we provide opportunities for them to grow in their faith and to claim their work as a beloved child of God.

Children and their experiences are valuable. Children are capable of wondering and reflecting as they grow in their faith. Children are not "other," to be silenced and ignored until they are adults. Children have wisdom that needs to be heard, affirmed, and shared. Every person is a full participant in the life of the faith community. Our stories impact our own faith journeys and the faith journeys of others. As children and adults reflect together on our experiences of God, we discover how God is at work in this world. Every person plays an important role in God's transformative work. Children are aware of God's presence and yearn to be connected to the Divine and to others. David Hay and Rebecca Nye call this a relational consciousness to God and to others.[5] Our relational connections strengthen and encourage us. One child reminded me: "God is still here . . . you do not see him . . . but he's here."

When we wonder together, children and I discover more about God and more about our relationship with God and others. Unfortunately, we rarely make time or space for children or for adults to do this holy work. We silence, push aside, or use children for the world's benefit. This normative understanding of children is oppressive and prevents children from growing in their faith and discovering ways to live their faith through love of God and neighbor. You've probably heard a child say something like one did to me, or else you thought it yourself when you were younger: "I do not like being the greeter on Sunday morning . . . all people do is pinch my cheeks and tell me how cute I am . . . I really don't like it." In response I asked: "I wonder what you like to do in church?" She answered, "I like to read and sing . . . when I do this people pay attention and listen . . . it makes me feel like my work is important."

Persons of all ages have gifts to share as they do God's work in the world. The church does not need children to act like little adults for them to be valuable members of the faith community. Our work is to help persons of all ages discover who they are as children of God and to help them uncover how they can participate in God's transformative work.

For this reason, my work as practical theologian is a quest for liberation and justice, a quest to develop a new understanding of humanity

---

4. Jensen, *Graced Vulnerability*, 2.
5. Hay and Nye, *Spirit of the Child*, 108.

that includes both children and adults. The quest for a new anthropological theology that informs and shapes faithful praxis and the field of Christian education begins with my experience of and with children. My hope is that by sitting with children, ministry leaders will discover that all persons, no matter their age, have an important role to play in God's work of transforming the world. My desire is to help persons develop a deep respect for God's youngest so that we can find ways to do the hard work of growing in our love of God and neighbor. My dream is that this intentional theological work will create a space where God and children together can answer big faith questions, providing insight that will lead to transformative change in the faith community.

How we understand God at work in the lives of all persons, regardless of age, has a direct impact on ministry and the work of a faith community. If we cling to the normative theological view that silences children, we risk missing God at work in the youngest members of our faith communities. God is actively present in the lives of all persons. A theology that does not value or listen to children shuts the door on all the holy possibilities for creativity that emerge out of the lives of these young people. When we actively listen to children, we experience God at work in their lives and in the lives of others. This strong personal conviction moves me to listen to children, to hear their stories, and to provide a space for them to tell me how they experience God. This truth pulls me forward towards a world where all people, regardless of their age, can be in a space where they can practice and live out their faith together.

My hope in writing this book is to help you, the reader, develop a deep theological understanding of God at work in children and a yearning to join in conversation with the children in your community. Through reflection on theology, scripture, and human and faith development, I hope to provide a strong basis for you to journey with and listen to children as an essential part of faith formation, theirs and yours.

The stories I heard from children and my experience in ministry with children and families guide us as we consider: "How is God at work in the lives of the youngest members of the body of Christ?" and "How am I, how are we, how is the church called to respond?" I hope this book will encourage you and give you the tools to listen to children, respect them as theologians, and encourage them as they grow in their faith. This is more important now than ever as we seek to discern what faith formation can and should look like in a COVID-19 reality and beyond. This work is essential in a world where inequality and lack of justice shadow our reality and limit our ability to live fully into God's beatific vision for God's good creation. Children are very aware of the anger that is expressed in the public. They overhear that people have been killed. They know people are protesting for hope, new life and inclusion. They worry about and they engage the world around them through the comments of their peers, their parents, the pastor's sermon, their teachers, and their own watching of news clips. They wonder about the anger and hate some show to others, they worry about name-calling, and they indeed do hope the world can be a place to welcome them, surround them and love them. May we discover God at work in and through persons of all ages, as we, the children in our midst, and the rest of our communities find ways to grow in our faith, responding to God's presence in our lives together.

RESEARCH BACKGROUND

As I sat with children and reflected on my experiences, several questions continued to challenge my faith and my work as a pastor in ministry with children:

- What can children teach faith leaders and communities about God and how we connect to the Divine?
- How does listening to children teach us about God and faith formation?
- How might children's stories about God shape our churches' religious education?
- How might children's insights transform the world?

These questions led to a nine-month research project, *Experiencing God Together*, in which I wondered with, listened to, and learned from twenty-eight different children. I first created a space where children felt safe to share their actual experiences with God. I realized that often children do not believe that adults really want them to speak or share their thoughts. Children become hyper-focused on providing what they think will be the correct answer ("Jesus?"), rather than answering from their life experience. I continually encouraged these twenty-eight children in their wondering. I let them know that I really wanted to hear about what they were thinking, and that their wonderings and discoveries would help me with my school project. As one astute child concluded: "So we are helping you with your homework." "Yes, I said. You are helping me with my homework. I am very curious to know what you are thinking." I will say more about the need and the process for creating a safe place in Chapter 3: Holy Conversation: Listening to Children.

I am grateful for the children who joined me on this journey and for those adults who supported them and encouraged them to participate. I worked at two different sites: the first was an afterschool program in a neighborhood church in Chicago, Illinois. Most of the sixteen children who attended were not members of this church, and indeed some do not participate in any type of faith community. Many of these children were from Hispanic cultures, and a few immigrated to the United States as infants or young children. These children ranged in age from six to twelve years. The second site was at an urban and culturally diverse church in downtown Chicago. The conversations took place in a traditional Sunday School classroom. Twelve children aged between five to twelve participated in these conversations. Each of these children came from a faith context, most of them United Methodist. I continue to be transformed by all of the children's theological wisdom and inspirational reflection. They taught me many things, including how they experience God.[6] Their wisdom continues to guide me in the work of faith formation and offers important insight as we imagine faith formation with children in this day and time.

BOOK OVERVIEW

I hope that as I share with you what I learned while working with these children, you likewise will develop your understanding of how children grow in their faith, and how they claim and respond to God's presence and love. Probably you will recognize your own church's children in the children I describe.

We begin this work in Chapter 2, where I claim that children are theologians. Children make meaning in response to their life experiences. They recognize and feel called to respond to the theological assertion that God is actively present in their lives and in the lives of others. Building

---

6. For a more detailed summary of the research methodology please see the Appendix: Research Methodology. It is also important to note that this project was fully reviewed by Human Subjects Research Committee (HSRC) at Garrett-Evangelical Theological Seminary.

on relational theology, I articulate an inclusive and liberating theology that honors God's transformational presence in the lives of children and advocates for the presence and work of children in all faith communities. This chapter focuses on the theological and scriptural foundation that engages children in reflection and helps them recognize God in their lives. I describe God as the good shepherd whose active presence guides persons of all ages in the holy work of transforming the world. I show that children have the capacity to connect with and respond to the Divine's presence in their lives. As one child shared: "God is always with us."

Chapter 3 builds on the theological and scriptural foundation established in Chapter 2 by describing how faith communities can create space for children and adults to wonder together, one learning from the other as they grow in their faith and strengthen their relationship with God. In this chapter, I assert that if we are not paying attention and listening to children, we risk not noticing God at work in our communities and our world. Wondering with and listening to children are two holy practices for all persons in ministry with children. How do those practices create space for us to hear God? We will consider how to create a space where all persons are welcomed, respected, and heard. Next, we will ponder how active wondering invites participants to consider different possibilities and to share their own reflections and insights. Finally, we will investigate how active listening invites children into the conversation, gives them space to listen to God, and encourages them to discern how to respond to all they are hearing and experiencing.

Chapter 4 considers children as theologians and reflects on their holy conversations with God. Using stories from ministry with children, this chapter describes the insights I gained by sitting with children as they worked to articulate their own understandings of the Divine. These stories reveal how children making meaning in response to their daily experiences through holy conversations with God and others. This is their theological work. That work includes engaging, recognizing, claiming, and responding to God's presence. Through this theological process, children reflect on their own experiences and deepen their faith and understanding of God.

Chapter 5 expands on the stories and insight shared in the previous chapters, describing the tools children use as they engage with God and neighbor. These six tools include: story, liturgy, relational awareness, memory markers (symbols, location, object), work, and wonder. These tools help persons enter into a relationship with the Holy and participate in the creative process of transforming the world. This chapter describes these tools and shares how the children use these tools in their meaning-making processes.

Chapter 6 considers how religious educators can use this information for faithful praxis in their communities. How can leaders in ministry with children encourage, nurture, and guide persons in their community as they pay attention, claim, and respond to God's presence in their lives? How can such leaders invite their entire community to respect the children in their community, listen to their wonderings, and include them in the life of the congregation? This chapter challenges you to find ways to welcome, listen to, wonder with, and work alongside the children in your community. It makes practical suggestions to encourage and equip you to create, nurture, and sustain an environment that not only welcomes children but listens to them, encourages them to wonder, guides them as they make new discoveries, and supports them as they respond to God's presence (and perceived absence) in their lives.

As you work through this book, think about how you listen to and wonder with children. How do you create a space in which children can practice using the spiritual developmental tools shared in Chapter 5? How do you encourage and equip your faith community to do this work alongside the children in your community? How do you keep the children in your community (those you have met and those who you have not yet met) in your thoughts and prayers? How do you help children and persons of all ages to engage in this holy work in your family or community? How have you witnessed persons in your family or faith community using these six tools? How does listening to and wondering with children provide insight and encouragement as you seek to lead ministry in new ways? How does your work with children shepherd them as they seek to build a world that ensures equality and justice for all? Hold on to your discoveries and celebrate how God is working in and through your children and faith community.

Next, ask yourself: "Where is there space in my ministry to introduce and practice using the tools that are currently absent in my community?" This will help you identify places where you can introduce, strengthen, practice, and develop these spiritual tools. Remember: faith formation is a process, a never-ending journey. We are always growing, learning new skills, and sharpening the tools we have for this holy work. One of the greatest gifts we can receive from and give to the children in our midst is the deep understanding that faith formation is an ongoing meaning-making process. We are continually engaging, recognizing, claiming, and responding to God every moment of every day. This is hard and holy work, and through it we and the world are transformed.

TOWARDS A PRACTICAL THEOLOGY AND MINISTRY WITH CHILDREN

When I first wrote this chapter, I was sitting in a space where there were children running, dancing, and playing all around me. Watching them were adults talking about the events of the day. Now, as I edit this chapter, I am six months into the COVID-19 pandemic. Currently, my interaction with children is through virtual tools including zoom. Some children play in the background as I participate in virtual meetings. Others attend worship, Vacation Bible School, and camp via zoom experiences I participate in. Whether physical or virtual, hearing the children's shrieks and the laughter, I find myself smiling, feeling the joy that comes from being surrounded by the ordinary and not so ordinary events of our life together. During this time, I had an opportunity to join children in a holy conversation via zoom. I asked them to participate in a scavenger hunt picking one item to show me and the rest of the group that reflected God's love during this time. One young child, eager to participate, ran up to the screen with a stuffed animal in hand: "Pastor Tanya, this is my favorite lovey. It's a pig. She reminds me that God loves me and keeps me safe." The ordinary and the extraordinary moments of life alongside theological, biblical, and developmental reflection continue to remind me of how, as Christian educator Dorothy Jean Furnish reminds us, the Bible is an encountering event and all are invited into the story, to experience the Holy, and to grow in the faith.

When we talk about faith formation and children's spirituality, we are pointing to a living faith—an active, growing, and changing reality in which persons experience and respond to God's grace and love moment by moment. A faithful practical theology of children therefore affirms this active process and guides children as they grow and live as disciples of Jesus Christ for the transformation of the world.[7] This holy work begins with a deep respect for children and a desire to create a nurturing space for children where they can participate as full members in the faith community.

---

7. This reflects the mission of the United Methodist Church: "to make disciples of Jesus Christ for the transformation of the world" (from *Book of Discipline*, 91.)

It affirms the value and sacred worth of children and encourages both imagination and critical thinking. Having children in my life pushes me to find or create faithful curricula that help shape and equip disciples for the transformation of the church and the world.

God is actively present in the lives of all children. God's grace moves in and through each of them. When we pay attention and act with care, we make meaning from our life experiences, and in so doing draw nearer to God and to neighbor. Such intimacy with God and neighbor motivates us to spread love wherever we go.

My experiences with children give me a deep respect for how the Divine is working in and through the youngest members of creation. Children have taught me that we are all called and equipped by our divine creator to journey together working towards the transformation of the world. We are called into a relationship built on mutual respect and trust. God's call to faithful ministry with children is not one that objectifies children. It does not focus on how children benefit me, other adults, or the entire faith community. Instead, ministry with children entails the entire faith community coming together to learn from and with one other. Therefore, God does not simply invite adults to pay attention to children, but demands that the church as a whole seek out ways to help children recognize, claim, and respond to God's presence in their lives.

May the stories, wisdom, and practical tools in this book help you determine how you can join children on this faith journey and how you can encourage and equip your faith communities to do the same. I pray that this book will equip you to create a space where adults and children together can experience God by engaging with our faith stories, recognizing God's presence, claiming God's grace, and responding to God's call to participate in the transformation of the world.

chapter 2

CHILDREN AS THEOLOGIANS

Making Meaning Together

> "God is still here . . . you do not see him . . . but he's here."
> —Anonymous (age 8)

It had been a long day. A group of confirmation participants (ages 11–12) and their adult mentors had traveled by van over five hours to our Methodist Conference Camp. As we were wrapping up the evening, an eleven-year-old boy bounced up to me and said, "I have a quick question." Thinking he wanted to know what was for breakfast or maybe what time we would wake them up in the morning, I said, "Alrighty. Ask away." He responded, "If God created everything, then who created God?" Shocked and overwhelmed by such a big question, I responded, "You know what, that's a great question. I need some time to think about it. Why don't we sleep on it and talk about it over breakfast tomorrow?" He responded: "Sure. Sounds great. G'night!!" And then he bounced joyfully off to bed.

I spent that night lying on the uncomfortable camp mattress trying to figure out how I was going to answer his question the next morning. How might I invite this child into a conversation that would affirm his wonderings and strengthen his faith? It was indeed a big question.

The next morning as I was piling scrambled eggs onto my plate, the boy bounced back up to me and announced, "I figured it out. No one created God. God just is." As I stood there holding my spoonful of eggs, I thought to myself, "and these are the moments when children teach me."

Each of us, as individuals who journey with children, have experiences with children with whom we are in ministry that challenge and teach us. Our experiences shape us, just as we hope and pray that the children's experiences in these moments shape their faith too. It is through holy conversation that we wonder, learn, and grow together. It is in these honest moments that we raise theological questions and search for deep theological meaning. Together, we engage in the work of theology. Together we make meaning in response to our own experiences. Together we grow closer to God and neighbor. Together we discover what God is calling us to do next.

We are all daily seeking to make meaning—to interpret—our experiences. We are trying to understand and interpret the events of our lives. Children, born with an innate sense of wonder and curiosity, participate in this work too. From birth, children use their senses to explore, discover, and grow. They do this work by paying attention, asking endless questions, and formulating language and conclusions that help them claim and share what they believe to be true.

Every child's community helps them in this work, beginning with their parents and caregivers. When we as ministry leaders are faithfully present to them, we have an opportunity to ask big questions, to model language as we reflect together, and to encourage children to consider what they want to do next. From the questions they ask ("I wonder where God lives?") to the statements they make ("God is with us when we are sad"), children try to respond to God as they find language to claim God's presence in their lives. While we might see these responses as cute and simple anecdotes to entertain others in their re-telling, what we as adults miss if we are not looking is that this is the child's attempt to make meaning, to find language with which to make sense of life. What could we say in response to the question about where God lives? What is driving the child's question? What is driving the child's assertion that God does not want us to be sad? How might we take seriously these attempts at making meaning?

Our work begins with us recognizing our own theological understanding of God with us. Claiming God's active presence in the lives of all people, no matter their age, establishes the foundation from whence we begin our work as those called into ministry with children. When we truly acknowledge "God with us" and "God with the children with whom we journey," we can begin our theological reflection together from a place of honor and respect recognizing our equality in Christ.

Next, we respond to God's presence in our lives and in the children's lives by meeting children where they are developmentally, socially, and spiritually. We recognize and claim how they learn and make meaning, seeking to understand the world around them. We provide opportunities for them to engage with the stories of our faith communities, and we invite them to consider their relationship to God by asking things like: "I wonder how you experienced God today?" We model spiritual language and spiritual disciplines. Then, we invite the children in our communities to practice alongside us as we reflect on God's presence and make meaning together.

This holy work provides every person in our community, no matter their age, a continuous opportunity to recognize, claim, and respond to God's presence in their lives. By seeking the Holy and responding out of love, we participate in all that God is doing and calling us to do for the transformation of the world. This is the divine dance in which God calls us to participate. This is how we interact with God and with one another, how we make meaning of God's presence in our lives, and how we discover ways to respond faithfully.

The question for us who journey with children is this: How can we invite, encourage, and support children as they participate in this trek alongside God and the rest of creation?

As adults who are in ministry with children, we must clarify and claim our role as shepherds and guides. Recognizing that we journey together shifts the pedagogical paradigm. No longer are we the knowledge carriers, depositing information into the young empty minds of the children in our community. Instead, we become models of the faith as we demonstrate what it looks like to wonder, to articulate our reflections, and to practice living out our faith in a chaotic world. Adults who journey with children as shepherds and guides encourage and show them how to make meaning in response to God's presence (and perceived absence) in their lives. In this journey or dance to make meaning together, we recognize that every person, no matter their age, has an opportunity to live as a theologian. Our role is to encourage and support this calling. Children, then, are theologians too, making meaning out of stories and their experiences of God. We do this holy work together.

Holy Work with Children

DISCOVERING GOD WITH US

We are all children of God, seeking to make meaning of our experiences as we claim and respond to God's presence in our lives. We begin this work by discerning our own theological understanding of God's presence in our lives. We must ask, "What does it mean to claim God with us? How does our understanding of God's presence affect our ministry with children?"

While there are many theologians who might shape and form our understanding of the theological assertion that "God is with us," each of us as individuals must walk our own path as we discover our own understanding of this theological claim. Children join us in this work and when we are all paying attention we can learn from and teach each other as we grow in our faith and find ways to live out our faith in a broken world.

It took me several years to formulate my own understanding of God's presence in my life and in the lives of others. As I write, I continue to tweak my assertions, taking care with every word. My education, my experiences, and my time spent in conversation with children have all offered me moments to engage in deep reflection as I consider what I believe and how those beliefs shape my praxis. Individuals of all ages have challenged me as I do this holy work.

I have had the privilege to listen to the reflections of others and to see persons of all ages grow in their theological reflection and their active faith. Through this work, it has become clear to me that each of us begins with our own personal understanding in response to our own experiences. When we open ourselves to conversation with and interaction in a faith community, then we can continue this work as we deepen and strengthen our faith. Age does not discriminate. When space is created and hearts are open, the Holy Spirit moves, and lives are changed as we make meaning together.

In order for us to join together in the meaning-making process, we begin with an attitude of respect for each individual, recognizing that each of us brings something to the conversation. The doctrine of prevenient grace provides a faithful starting place for doing this work together. Prevenient grace, in a Wesleyan understanding, affirms that God is actively present in the lives of all people at all times. God's love and offer of relationship comes before any human action and provides the invitation and foundation for a deep connection between creation and the divine creator. This divine love exists and surrounds all of God's creation—young and old alike. From the beginning, children are wrapped in God's unending, unmerited, and eternal love for them. This theological understanding provides the foundation for our work with ministry with children. We begin with a recognition of God's presence in each of our lives. Therefore, our work is not to give someone God's love, but instead, to help the individuals with whom we are in ministry recognize, claim, and respond to God's presence and love in their lives.

This truth is revealed and affirmed through the sacrament of Holy Baptism.[1] Through baptism, the church acknowledges God's actions, God's grace, and God's love for each person. We affirm God's active presence in the life of every person, no matter their age. In many protestant traditions, during the Sacrament of Baptism, we also commit to surrounding the persons being baptized with love and forgiveness as they grow in their service to others. We covenant to pray for the individual so that they might live as a true disciple of Jesus Christ. With this communal covenant, we claim the call to support one another with Christian love. Again, a communal picture is drawn, where people of all ages gather to learn, to wonder, to grow, and to share together. We begin with the theological claim of God's presence and love in our lives, and then we work together to live out that love in all times and places, making a difference in the world around us. Therefore, our meaning-making process does not end with a deeper understanding of God. Instead, when we truly recognize and claim God's presence in our lives, we want to respond, sharing God's love with others. The meaning-making process therefore is one that begins with reflection and leads to faithful action.

Throughout my ministry, I witness children not only engaging with the theological understanding of Christ with us but I am privileged to see how they take it a step further as they wrestle with how to live out that theological understanding in their lives. This is the holy work to which we are called as we recognize and claim "God with us." This is how each of us shows up as a theologian and discerns how God is calling us to participate in this world. Children, like adults, are actively participating in this meaning-making process as they respond to God's grace and love in their lives. We do this work together.

---

1. United Methodist Church, *Book of Worship*, 95–105.

THE DIVINE DANCE: MAKING MEANING TOGETHER

Thankfully, we do not do this work alone. God is with us from the beginning, and God moves with us throughout the multiplicities of possibilities with which life presents us. Theologian Marjorie Suchocki describes God's work in and through the world using the image of a kaleidoscope as a metaphor.[2] Suchocki argues that the creative work of the divine and of creation reflects the multiple pieces held in the image seen in the toy. The world is full of possibilities with various experiences and outcomes. With just a touch, all the pieces (all the possibilities) shift and a new image can be seen.[3] With just one small decision, the whole world can shift to have an impact on the rest of creation. "God who is with us and for us," offers a relational presence that moves with creation through the shifts of life.[4] God moves in and through all of these shifts and changes, calling humanity forward towards God's hope for creation.

Moving through the kaleidoscope of life, God creates out of love, trust, and hope, entering into faithful relationship with humanity. As we seek to make meaning, God calls us towards our purpose, our right path, and our work for the transformation of the world. This is true no matter the age of the disciple. Each of us, no matter our age or stage in life, plays a part in the unfolding of God's beatific vision, allowing God's call to work in and through us as we support each other in transformative work.

In her book, *Dancing with God*, Karen Baker-Fletcher describes this holy movement as a divine dance in which the triune God and humanity move and participate together in the unfolding of creation. "The Holy Spirit inspires the dance of God, calling all to participate in the dance of divine love, creativity, healing, justice, and renewal."[5] Using invitational language, Baker-Fletcher describes the work of the Trinity as persuasive and relational. God invites and persuades creation into a healing relationship, drawing "humankind toward positive possibilities and a realization of true creative potential."[6] When we participate in this dance together alongside the Holy Spirit, we discover what to do next—or as children teach me, we know how to respond. In this understanding, we, alongside

---

2. Suchocki, *God, Christ, Church*, 3–4.
3. Suchocki, *God, Christ, Church*, 3–4.
4. Suchocki, *God, Christ, Church*, 36.
5. Baker-Fletcher, *Dancing with God*, 163.
6. Baker-Fletcher, *Dancing with God*, 49.

Children as Theologians

God, and the children with whom we are in ministry, are co-creators, working with the Divine for creative transformation of personal lives, social structures, and global realities.

It is important to note that we show up for the dance and do this work wherever we are on a given day and at a given time. Therefore, a two-year-old might show up full of wonder and curiosity, eagerly repeating the words of the story or the words of the storyteller. An eight-year-old might show up with questions and concerns as they wrestle to understand the linear details of the story. Adolescents might bring more developed abstract thinking and begin to wonder how the story impacts their identity and their work in the world. We each bring our own experiences and tools to the table. We each bring different movements and different speeds. For this reason, it is good to pay attention to the children with whom we are in ministry, recognizing their developmental, social, and spiritual stages. We must honor where they are in their age and stage of life. When we pay attention and invite these children to show us who they are and who God is calling them to be, then we can encourage and support them in the holy work of showing up faithfully in the creative dance.

Faithful ministry with children must therefore recognize how every child is called and equipped to participate fully in God's beatific vision. Children are not simply observers, adults in the making, or persons who should be cast aside until they are older. Instead, every person is a full participant in all that God is doing for the transformation of the world.

Yet our work is not only to recognize God in our midst, but to find ways to understand and respond to this presence. This is the meaning-making process for which we were created and to which we are called. As we do this holy work, we discover God in our midst, and our hearts yearn for ways to respond. This is the divine dance into which each person, no matter their age, is called—seeking meaning, developing understanding, and responding faithfully. Through this dance, each person has an opportunity to participate alongside God and the rest of creation in the work of transforming the kingdom, which is the work of sharing God's light and love with others. In the Christian tradition, we look to God and community to help us in this work.

Children do this work too as they wonder, ask questions, learn from those in their community, and discover their own thoughts and feelings in response to their life experiences. For this reason, questions are a natural part of our faith formation process. No matter our age, we reflect on our experiences and try to interpret them in search of meaning and deeper understanding. This is fundamental to the work of recognizing and responding to God's presence and love. No matter our age, we are called into this dance.

This theological assertion grounds us in our ministry with children. It drives our questions: How do we invite, encourage, teach, and guide children into this holy work? How can we help children recognize, claim, and respond to God's grace and love?

Conversations with children create space for each of us to participate in theological discourse together. When we abstain from simply giving children information, when we avoid the top-down pedagogical approach of merely telling children *about* God, then we can create a holy space for persons of all ages to encounter God and make meaning together. We do this work in community, each guiding the other. Through the wondering and active listening of holy conversation, we learn and grow together. By sharing stories, modeling language, and inviting children to wonder and discover, we encourage and guide them to discover God in their lives and to find ways to respond to God's grace and love.

Observe the flow of the dance, this give and take as each participant responds to the other. As the adults in the room, we might take the lead in some instances, and in others, we follow where the younger disciples lead us. When we truly listen to one another, opportunities arise for us not only to teach, but to learn. And don't we still want to learn? It is through this divine dance that we discover the ways in which God is calling us and the children with whom we are in ministry to be light in the world.

THE GOOD SHEPHERD: A PEDAGOGICAL MODEL FOR OUR WORK TOGETHER

Living in the midst of a global pandemic, watching a black man murdered on TV, hearing and participating in riots and protests, and experiencing political divisiveness—it is no wonder our children are asking: "Why are people so mean to one another?" "Why would they kill him just because of the color of his skin?" And as one adolescent reflected: "We can do better. We have to do better!" Our children live in a broken world that is ever changing. They are aware of and impacted by these realities and so many more. How can we encourage them as they continue to experience and respond to God's presence and love in the midst of all the difficulties life presents? This is what I call hard and holy work, and it is essential that as leaders in ministry with children we are intentional as we guide and model this dance for others.

One biblical image that I find helpful in this work is that of the Good Shepherd as described in Psalm 23. This beloved Psalm introduces us to the one who leads and guides us on the good and proper path. The imagery and promises of this text offer comfort to many through a metaphor that describes how God participates in creation as a relational effective presence. We see a shepherd who cares for his sheep, who is focused on providing for and protecting the flock. We hear promises of goodness, peace, and happiness in the midst of life's chaotic and often disappointing and tragic flow. The Hebrew text describes a shepherd who leads or guides, leading the psalmist "in proper paths" (Ps 23:3 CEB). The imagery of the psalmist's poetry provides us with a vision of a shepherd faithfully and carefully leading the sheep, with the promise and hope that "goodness and faithful love will pursue me all the days of my life" (Ps 23:6 CEB). Following the Good Shepherd, following God, leads to life. In responding to the Shepherd's call, "come follow me," we are not promised that all will work out well, but instead we are assured that we do not walk alone. With the Good Shepherd as our guide, we will find a way to move through the kaleidoscope of all of life's events and will discover and experience happiness in the midst of life's uncertainties.

Jesus builds on this metaphor of the Good Shepherd in both the Gospels of Matthew and John. In the parable of the lost sheep (Matt 18:12–14) and the parable of the Good Shepherd (John 10:1–16) Jesus affirms the Old Testament metaphor of God as one who leads and guides. Jesus confirms that God is the Good Shepherd who is actively present in the lives of each sheep, working as guide to protect each individual sheep and the entire flock. In the parable of the lost sheep, as told in the Gospel of Matthew, the author presents God as the shepherd who knows and cares for every sheep. This is an example we do well to follow in our ministry; our work begins by counting each sheep and calling them by name. In my work, I have met many children from many different places, with many different names, with many different pronunciations. Several of the children I worked with in Chicago would introduce themselves saying: "My real name is Aksana, but if that is too hard to pronounce, you can call me Ana." I would immediately respond: "What would you like me to call you? I would like to learn how to pronounce your real name if that is what you prefer to go by." And then a conversation and learning opportunity would ensue, these young disciples teaching me, me learning new languages and new pronunciations. It served as a beginning to a relationship, one that is built on a foundation of respect and one that moves in response to an invitation for each of us to guide and learn from the other. It is holy work, fashioned and shaped by our shepherd and loving guide.

This work to follow in the Good Shepherd's footprints down the good and proper path, takes intentionality and care. It requires relationships built on respect. This takes time and patience as we learn to trust one another. "I am the Good Shepherd. I know my own and my own know me" (John 10:14 NRSV). In the Gospel of John's description of the Good Shepherd, Jesus describes an intimate relationship in which the shepherd knows the sheep by name, and in return is known and trusted by the flock: "The sheep hear his voice. He calls his own sheep by name and leads them out. When he has brought out all his own, he goes ahead of them, and the sheep follow him because they know his voice" (John 10:3a–5 NRSV). This parable speaks of trust, recognizing the sheep's reluctance to follow a stranger. The sheep know whom they can trust and they follow faithfully. As John B. Cobb and David Ray Griffin argue, "trusting God is not assurance that whatever we do, all will work out well. It is instead confidence that God's call is wise and good."[7] The sheep must trust the shepherd, having confidence in God's call and leadership. This is essential if the sheep is to faithfully follow the shepherd. Here, trust does not equate with the sheep blindly following the shepherd. Instead the sheep follows because the shepherd is trustworthy and good.

This is how we show up in the divine dance together: building relationships, developing trust, guiding and following. There is a give and take, an ebb and flow that is necessary for this authentic work to unfold. It requires, time, presence, respect, and commitment. This is our work: before we even begin to think about what curriculum we will teach, what lessons we want to share, and what learning goals we want to accomplish, we must create a community built on respect and trust. We can do this work when we follow the lead of our Good Shepherd, taking care with our presence as an adult in the sacred space. As one child once said: "You are the big person here, you are in charge."

We must hold our power and authority with respect and care. Often when people attempt to describe God's presence in the world, they use

---

7. Cobb and Griffin, *Process Theology*, 158.

language of persuasion or describe God as one who lures another towards the most beneficial outcome. While this might be a helpful way of understanding God's effective presence in the world, we must move with care as we identify language that helps us faithfully join with children in the meaning-making process. Language of persuasion or the act of luring suggests a relationship built on coercion. It is easy, as the individuals with power and authority, to step into the role of the enforcer—one who lures, persuades, and in some instances forces a child to do something. Unless someone is in real danger, these tactics are often not helpful and can be harmful in our work to build transparent community where we learn and grow together. Relationships that are coercive are built on fear, not trust.

Instead, the image described in Psalm 23, and the Gospels' parables, describe a God who creates and actively participates in the lives of all persons without micromanaging, manipulating, or forcing one to act in a specific way. God moves in the world through trust, love, and hope. God does not demand, manipulate, nor does the Divine force persons to move. Free will prevails, and choice exists. This description reflects a healthy, loving, and nurturing relationship. Following Christ's example, we can uncover a more faithful approach to our work as the responsible adult in this holy space. Our role is to follow the Good Shepherd's example as we guide, lead, encourage, and support the sheep in our flock. The Good Shepherd guides the sheep and promises to be with them through all of the shifts and changes in life. This reflects a healthy, safe, and loving relationship. A relationship that is built on love, trust, and hope, not on fear. A relationship that is not a response to manipulation or coercion, but instead that invites humanity to trust, and to follow. As one of my professors, Dr. Stephen Ray, once stated: "God is closer to us than our heartbeat, guiding us in love, and hope." This relational and effective presence is revealed in the words and reflections of the young theologians who teach me: "He shows the sheep where to go." "The Good Shepherd loves the sheep." "We can trust the Good Shepherd." Following Christ's model as shepherd, we can offer the spiritual guidance that children need as they develop their faith language.[8] This is indeed our calling and our work—to be present, to listen, and to build trust as we guide and lead the children with whom we are in ministry as they seek to make meaning and find their place in the divine dance.

---

8. Caldwell, *I Wonder*, loc. 766.

CONCLUDING THOUGHTS

The model the Good Shepherd gives us is one of authentic relationship, a relationship in which we begin by claiming the value found in every person who comes to the table, praying for those who are missing, and welcoming each sheep when they arrive. When I work with children, I intentionally create a time at the beginning and at the end of our designated schedule for us to sit with one another, listening and sharing. As children gather, I greet them by name and say: "I am so glad you are here! Welcome to our circle." Then, I engage in conversation asking: "I wonder what happened this week that you want to share?" Nearing the end of our time together as we gather for prayers, I ask: "I wonder what made you happy this week? I wonder what made you sad this week?" Finally, as our time together ends, I ask them: "I wonder what you are most excited about? I do hope you will tell me about it when we are together again." Then, the next time we are together I make sure to ask them about their experience. Following each of these questions is space and time for every child to respond. I tell children that if they do not feel comfortable speaking out loud, they can always come and tell me later, or they can just hold their thoughts quietly, knowing God hears them. While it takes time to develop a consistent flow of conversation, my experience has shown that when I am intentional in creating the space, within three to four weeks children begin to trust that I do really want to hear their thoughts—and that is when the deeper and more authentic conversation begins to emerge.

This promise of the Good Shepherd as provider, protector, and guide, is a gift to us and to the children with whom we are in ministry. We can cling to God as shepherd as we respond to God's call to teach and guide the youngest members of our faith community. We can also follow God's example as we guide our flock. We can become shepherds to the children in our care. When we recognize God's presence in our lives and the lives of our ministry partners, and when we respond by creating a space built on respect and trust that invites children to share their experiences of this presence through active wondering and listening, we create an opportunity for people of all ages to participate together in the divine dance and make meaning and respond with love together.

God is present in the lives of children guiding them as full participants in the divine dance and the transformation of the world. Children are an essential part of God's work in creation—at every age and stage of their life journeys. If we are not paying attention to children—and if we are not showing them how to pay attention to God—then we risk missing God at work in the world. The task at hand then is to create a space where persons can share their stories and reflect on their experiences with God as they discern how they are feeling called to respond. We turn to this work in Chapter 3.

chapter 3

HOLY CONVERSATION

Listening to Children

"I wonder . . . how do I know I believe in God?" —Anonymous (age 4)

"That is a big question, you know I wonder about that too . . . maybe we can discover ways to do this work together." —Pastor Tanya

OUR CALL TO MINISTRY WITH CHILDREN

In Chapter 1, I introduced you to the young boy who asked, "How do I know I believe in God?" Looking back on this experience, I could tell from the adults' body postures, facial expressions, and comments that they were hoping I would be able to provide an answer to their son's question. I remember getting down on eye level with this young person and seeing the curiosity in his eyes as he anticipated my answer. Hoping to acknowledge the importance of what he was asking, I responded: "That is a big question, I wonder about that too." It was in this moment that I learned and experienced the importance of open wondering and conversation. Little did I know that this conversation was preparing me for future work and a time when I would talk with another child during the COVID-19 global pandemic as she asked: "I wonder why God is letting all of this happen?" Followed shortly by a different conversation with another child in response to George Floyd's death: "Why do people who say they believe in God treat each other this way?"

What followed each of these questions was a conversation where we wondered together. "I don't know," I honestly responded to each of these children. "I wonder about that too." Then, to the child asking about

COVID-19 and God's presence I asked: "I wonder what we know about God that can help us during this hard time?" This young girl thought for a moment and said: "I know that God loves me and that God is with me. I am praying God helps our world heal and stay healthy." We continued in conversation together celebrating God's presence and love while sharing our grief and sadness too. The conversation with the young child about humankind, evil, and racism was admittedly harder. I had to take a breath and really think and process the possibilities before continuing. "That is a really big question," I responded. I wonder what you think God is feeling?" "I think God is sad . . ." This young child responded. After a short pause ". . . and angry." "Hmmmm," I responded. "Those are big and important feelings." "I wonder how you are feeling?" We continued the conversation and talked about our feelings and what we can do when we feel those big feelings. We ended our time together wondering about what God is asking us to do. "I think God is calling me to be kind and share love with everyone," this young child shared honestly. "That is big and important work," I affirmed. "I'm grateful God has you and others to do this work during this important time."

Did I answer these children's questions? Maybe. Maybe not. I have come to understand my job is to be more about listening, modeling language, and encouraging curiosity as children discover their own answers to the really big questions life creates. For many of these questions do not have simple answers. It is a life long journey that helps us uncover and claim our own understanding of how God moves in and through our lives. In this moment, my hope was to acknowledge each of the children's questions, to claim the call to curiosity and wonder, and to practice active listening as we learned from one another. My goal was not to provide a quick answer or to solve the problem, but my hope was to affirm their questions and encourage their meaning-making process. My role was to guide these children as they did the important work of engaging life questions, claiming God's presence, and identifying how such moments help us strengthen our faith in God.

When we wrestle to understand, we are not looking for someone to give us "the" answer. We are seeking a conversation partner to journey with us as we grow in our own awareness and belief. As leaders in ministry with children, a majority of our role is to create space, to encourage curiosity, to listen, and to affirm. We begin this work with a deep respect for the ones with whom we are in ministry. Through relational ministry, we create space for children to share their experiences and to wonder as they make their own discoveries. In essence, our work begins with a call to hear from the children themselves. We cannot know what they seek or discover what they know if we do not listen first.

Participating in God's divine dance together reveals a call to ministry with children where we as adults show up differently, where we create a space for children to wonder, discern, and reflect together. This dance requires a deep respect and a willingness not simply to provide an answer, but to encourage and guide all persons as they do the hard and holy work of faith formation. Our task is to create a safe space where children feel welcome and safe to investigate the many facets of faith with us. Our work is guided by active wondering and listening—the process of asking big questions as we create space for persons of all ages to discern, discover, and respond. Active wondering with and listening to children become two holy practices for all persons in ministry with children.

These are the tools God provides us for rich and faithful ministry with children. As leaders in ministry with children, it is essential that we clean and sharpen these tools. So they do not grow dull or become rusted, we use them continually. In this chapter we will consider how to:

- create a safe space where children and adults show up openly and honestly
- engage in active wondering and listening as we discern what God is calling us to do next.

Using these tools, we can create a safe space for children and adults to reflect, share, wonder, and learn together as each individual and the community grows in their faith and strengthens their relationships with God. The task at hand then is to create a space where persons can share their stories and reflect on their experiences with God as they discern how they are feeling called to respond.

MY EXPERIENCE: QUALITATIVE RESEARCH WITH CHILDREN

Much of what I have learned comes out of my experience leading ministry with children in multiple cities, states, and countries too. Over the last twenty years, I have come to see creating a safe space, active wondering, and active listening as significant tools for this important work. This work has taught me that a faithful and practical theology for ministry with children must rise out of the stories of children. When we listen well, we can hear what God is saying to us and to them.

Recognizing the need to wonder and listen with children, in the fall of 2013, I began to craft a qualitative research project in which I would invite children to wonder and discover with me. I hoped that in and through this process we would connect to God, and that through their reflections the children would teach me how they experience and respond to God's presence in their lives. My goal? To create a space where children felt welcome and safe to investigate with me the many facets of faith. In pursuit of this goal, I created a nine-month research project, *Experiencing God Together*, in which I wondered with, listened to, and learned from twenty-eight different children.

In setting up this project, I partnered with two different churches. The first church partner was a large urban downtown church with a diverse staff and multi-cultural congregation. While predominantly white, a few of the children were Filipino and Latino. I led my research project during the traditional Sunday School hour on Sunday mornings in between the church's two worship services. The second church partner was an afterschool program located in a smaller urban neighborhood church. The children ranged in age from six to twelve years of age. None of these children were members at this neighborhood church. Each child came from a different faith background too. This group was predominately Hispanic. Many of these children either immigrated to the States with their parents, or they are the first child in their families born in the United States. For the majority of these children, English is their second, if not third or fourth language. While the children all chose to speak to me in English, a Spanish translator worked alongside me when I met with them, their families, and the community. Following Jerome Berryman's *Godly Play* model, the children and I gathered weekly and moved through a liturgy of gathering, getting ready, hearing a story, wondering about the story, responding to the story through various art options, feast, and then the final blessing.[1]

The entire project took nine months to create, implement, and analyze. Prior to beginning the project, I met with church leadership, parents, and the children. My goal was to build relationships with each of these individuals in a way that increased the likelihood of authentic feedback

---

1. It is important to note that the work of Jerome Berryman and the *Godly Play* Curriculum is essential to me as a religious educator. Valuing this method, I used Berryman's liturgy and stories to create a safe space to have holy conversation. I am grateful for his scholarship and contribution to ministry with children.

throughout the research project. I spent four months working and volunteering in these two communities with these children as a way to develop a relationship with them prior to the official start of the project. Many people asked: "How do you expect to get substantial answers from the children in this project?" My answer every time was: "By building relationships and creating safe space." I knew that if I showed up as an authentic adult, over time the children and I would begin to trust one another and honest conversation would follow. Children provide simple or inauthentic answers if/when they do not trust the person who is asking the question, or if they think that their peers will judge or shame them for their answers. Building a safe community takes time and intentional work.

The other step I knew was essential in creating an authentic and safe space was to create a liturgy through which children could come to know what to expect every time they came into the research space. This is where the liturgy, the flow of our time together, became so important. Each week we followed the same flow of events, providing structure and consistency to our time together. Each week I could see the children relaxing as they shared a little more of their reflections with me and the entire group. By the end of our time together, it was clear that the children trusted me, the other adults, and their peers enough to engage in honest and authentic conversation.

Over the course of these nine months I began to experience what somewhere deep down I knew to be true: when we do the holy work of setting the space well, children blossom as they show up with honesty and authenticity. Their answers developed from short one word answers: "Yes," "No," "I don't know," "because," and the famous church answer, "Jesus," into deep reflections as they shared how they felt when they are sitting in worship listening to music, what their hopes are for their family, and what they pray for every night knowing God is listening. Many of the children in the diverse and multi-cultural after school program group would often reflect on and share wisdom gained from extended family members (Grandparents, aunts, uncles as well as parents and siblings too) as well as cross-cultural experiences. "When we first came here I was scared, my aunt told me that we were doing this together. She helped me remember I am not alone."

Through these holy conversations, I began to understand how these children claim God's presence and find ways to respond to God's grace and love. I am grateful for the children who joined me on this journey and for those adults who supported them and encouraged them to participate.

Seven years later, I continue to be transformed by their theological wisdom and inspirational reflection. They taught me many things, including how they experience God. My theology was defined and clarified by joining in conversation with children five to twelve years old.

While I initially set out to learn more about how children recognize, claim, and respond to God's grace and love, as I continue to reflect on this project, I can now see the wisdom held in the process as I recognize the steps taken that opened up conversation and led to wonder and discovery. I can now see how the intentional process I created led to children opening up and sharing with adults and their peers. Each of these learnings has value and each impacts our work as we participate in ministry with children by listening to, affirming, and supporting them. This work begins with each of us intentionally creating safe space for those with whom we are in ministry, and then requires us to wonder and listen to those who join us in these holy conversations. When we engage in holy discourse with whom we are in ministry, space opens for us to discern: God, what are you saying to us today? Where are you leading us as we attempt to gain understanding of our relationship with you and with each other? I have learned that individuals of all ages are capable of this work.

EMBRACING THE CALL TO CREATE A SAFE SPACE FOR WONDER AND DISCOVERY

Human and faith development theories highlight the importance of developing trust and a sense of security in the early stages of human development. John Bowlby, in his work with infants and attachment, notes the importance of a child developing a secure attachment with a parent or caregiver as a way to develop a sense of safety and security. He argues that this foundational work has far-reaching implications for relationship health and satisfaction, well into adolescence and adulthood.[2] Erik Erikson human development theorist also argues for the need to develop an unconscious trustworthiness in self and others. The hope for Erikson is that a child develops this basic trust within the first year of life.[3]

James Fowler, a professor and United Methodist minister, also worked to understand how persons find meaning from their lives. Fowler's theory of faith development encompasses six stages and one pre-stage that

---

2. Newman and Newman, *Theories of Human Development*, 28.
3. Erikson, *Identity and the Life Cycle*, 57.

potentially occur throughout an individual's lifespan. The pre-stage, described as infancy and undifferentiated faith, is characterized by an infant's realization that while they are separate beings they rely on others to meet their needs. In this stage, individuals begin to develop a sense of trust. Ideally, as individuals develop, they gain a clear understanding and trust in themselves, in others, and ultimately in the Divine through their encounters with the world around them. People learn to trust others and God in response to their relationships and social interactions.[4]

For each of these theorists, trust becomes a foundation on which relationships are built. Fowler helps us see the connection between human relationships and relationships with the Divine. As children learn to trust their caregivers and themselves, realizing that they can fulfill their essential needs and thus ensure their survival, they begin to understand the world around them as a safe place to explore. In other words, when we feel safe and trust the ground underneath us, we can dance freely.

And yet, we know that the world is not always a safe place, and that not all spaces are safe for wondering and discovery. All too often, spaces created for children are filled with adults who seek to provide information, answers, and their adult version of truth. Adults show up with an egocentric focus, feeling good that they are showing up to teach the children, but inevitably they miss the mark when they fail to pay attention to, listen to, and learn from the young members of the body of Christ. Following Paulo Freire, I often refer to this model of education as banking pedagogy for it assumes that by depositing information into a young person's brain it will have an impact on the child. This approach to learning developed out of a rich history of Christian education. During the 1820s–1880s a sense of urgency developed, moving the church to focus on evangelism and the conversion of others to Christ.[5] This movement sought after the ideals of human betterment and salvation. Often referred to as the Sunday school movement, this ecological shift between 1840 and 1912 resulted in the creation of Sunday Schools throughout the nation. This form of education focused on transferring knowledge, and therefore the curriculum focused on lecturing, memorization, and tests.

More than one hundred years later, many religious educators are still focused on the transference of knowledge, attempting to *give* children the faith instead of working with them to nurture the spiritual presence that is already

---

4. Fowler, *Stages of Faith*, 120.
5. Boys, *Educating in Faith*, 27.

in them. Many publishers create uniform lessons that are displayed in an attractive manner, inviting ministry leaders simply to pick up the material and use it with little to no preparation or forethought. Intentionality is often lost in the drive to have access to information quickly and without much effort. Technology fuels this desire as we search for instant knowledge. We launch into doing, omitting the sustaining work of being. We move quickly from task to task, lesson to lesson, without forethought or space for reflection. Life happens and we move on without ever taking an opportunity to relish the moment and soak up God's presence, grace, and love.

When we simply provide Christian education for children, we ignore this call for intentionality, and we bypass opportunities for developing wonder and encouraging discovery. We forget that faith is a life-long process, we neglect the call to help people of all ages develop their own capacities for spiritual formation, and we abandon the call for relational ministry of any kind. Banking pedagogy therefore contributes to an oppressive narrative, one that is built on giving persons faith and telling them what to believe instead of creating a space where the Holy Spirit can move freely, helping persons develop their individual faith narratives in relationship with others through active wondering, critical thinking, reflection, and discovery.

As leaders in ministry with children, we have a different model, a different path for life long faith formation. For us, building a religious community includes creating a space in which children can share their stories, practice wondering, use their imaginations, and learn from the entire community. Spiritual development reflects the personal dimension of learning that nurtures spiritual growth by providing a space for the faith to become "embodied in each person." This leads persons to work together in communities; it calls "persons into relationship, friendship, care, and justice with others and the creation." The "starting point for education is the person."[6]

Nurturing spiritual growth in children includes recognizing their inner spark, the Divine presence in each child. It also involves nurturing the spiritual growth process, and guiding all children as they make meaning from their experiences and relationships. Spiritual growth honors the individual child and affirms their particular developmental process. Finally, religious instruction is the "formal process of theological reflection, of teaching and learning, where we come to know, interpret, and incarnate the faith."[7] It is in this intentional space that teachers and children share the faith stories with

6. Seymour, *Mapping Christian Education*, 19–20.
7. Seymour, *Mapping Christian Education*, 19–20.

each other, engage in intentional theological reflection, and use developmentally appropriate pedagogical methods that help every person learn, make meaning, and respond to their experience with the Holy.

CREATING A SAFE SPACE

In our work as leaders in ministry with children, we demonstrate a different and more fruitful model of how to engage faithfully in ministry with children. We do this by creating a safe space where children are valued and respected, and by inviting them into the process of learning through claiming and responding to God's presence in their lives.

Practicing Respect

Our work begins with a deep respect for the children with whom we are in ministry and a desire to create a space where all our welcomed, respected, and heard. Instead of merely "imparting knowledge," we build relationships, get to know the children in our communities, and provide opportunities for them to discover and share who they are as beloved children of God. Our work does not involve forcing our ideas, thoughts, or desired behaviors on those with whom we are in ministry simply because they are younger. We can share our thoughts and model best practices as we enter into a holy conversation with those we journey alongside. We claim the divine presence in each of the children we will meet, and we grow closer to God and neighbor through this holy work.

In my conversation with that young boy many years ago, before responding I grounded myself, asking God to give me the words as I invited this young person into conversation. I began our conversation by saying: "You know, our church believes that these conversations are so important that they hired me, a pastor with children, to join you in these conversations. You can ask me anything, anytime you want." This was my attempt to open the space, affirm my respect for this child and invite him into authentic conversation. I have learned over the years that the best leader to engage in this work is one who honors each child, strives to get to know them, and seeks to join them in their life long faith process.

Part of building respect is creating space to get to know each child while paying attention to how their culture and community impacts what they feel, experience, and do. Cultural awareness is essential as we strive to learn more about and build relationships with our children. We are shaped by our community, our culture, and our experiences. For this reason, as a researcher and leader in ministry with children I value the opportunity to get to know each individual child as they reveal who they are as shaped and formed by their own wonderings and experiences. We build respect by asking each child to show us who they are as they share their culture and experiences with us. We learn and grow as children teach us about who they are and the things that are important to them. Children shape our understanding when we create space and are open to all they have to teach us about their unique realities and experiences.

It is also important that we train and equip our adult leaders in safe practices as they model respect and care for the children with whom they are in ministry. For when we engage in ministry with children, we adults bring with us a certain amount of power and authority by the very nature of our role as the adult in the room. The children look to us to keep them safe. And so we must hold our power and authority carefully. How do we show this? By avoiding any actions that feel or appear to be coercive or manipulative. By offering children choices, listening when they speak, and encouraging them as they learn how to be in community with others.

Finally, it is well to recall that we do ourselves and the children a deep disservice if we are lax about finding good teachers. They need far more than a "warm body" to teach them. Through prayerful discernment, we can find persons truly called and gifted for this work. This is an essential step in creating safe spaces—identifying and supporting adults who value and respect children and want to shepherd them in the holy work of their spiritual formation.

Getting Ready

We show our respect through our actions and our words. This begins before children even arrive in the space we are creating. We show respect to the children with whom we are in ministry by taking the time necessary to prepare thoroughly, to get our bodies and our space ready. Leaders who rush into a room without the proper supplies or plans are simply filling a role, just doing something, instead of striving to create a meaningful learning space. This is where most ministries fail: rushing to the objective, moving quickly through a curriculum, and not taking time to invite all into the process.

We get our bodies ready through prayer and preparation. We might choose to:

- Pray before we enter into our ministry space, asking God to help us in this holy work.
- Pray over the ministry space, asking God to move in and through our time with the children in a way that is encouraging and life giving to all.
- Pray for each child and their family by name.

However we ground ourselves and prepare for the work ahead, we are intentional in beginning our work well, acknowledging the call, and asking God to guide us in our work. We make sure the classroom is set and ready: i.e., that the curriculum has been reviewed and thoughtfully planned, and that all supplies are gathered prior to the start time of the ministry setting. This enables us to be fully present when the children arrive.

Practicing Presence

Once we are ready, we show up and practice the gift of presence by greeting children at the door, welcoming them to the space, and inviting them to participate in the gathering. This is an important opportunity to greet every child by name, or to ask their name if you do not yet know it. This is where relationship building begins. As we practice presence we have an opportunity to ease any concern the child or their caregivers might have. This also gives the child time to observe the classroom and to find peace before they enter into the new space. As children become accustomed to the space and to our greeting, they will likely look forward to greeting and sharing things with us too. This is a wonderful time to connect and show that we care about them and their experiences.

I meet children at the door, often kneeling down or sitting to greet them at eye level, introduce myself, and invite them to join the others inside. For example, this is what I might say on a given day:

> Greeting: "Hi [name]. My name is Tanya, and I am one of your leader(s) today. I am excited that you are here."
>
> Invitation: "I invite you to find a seat in the circle/a chair at the table that looks good to you" (depending on room setup).

Through the greeting and invitation, we give children specific instructions as to where to go and what to do. This creates a clear pathway for them to follow as they enter the space, and it minimizes any confusion or anxiety.

Some children will not be ready to enter the classroom immediately. Make them comfortable as they decide whether or not to enter. If a child is not ready to enter into the space or to leave their parents/caregivers, you can say, "Sometimes it's hard to get ready," or "I see that you are not ready to come into this new space." Then follow with an invitation, "You can sit next to me and watch as you get your body ready." As children grow comfortable with the idea of entering into a new space, encourage their parents/caregivers to stay outside the space with the child until that child feels comfortable and safe to enter the space on their own.

GATHERING

While the adult at the door greets the children and invites them into the space you have created, additional leaders can help the incoming children find their seats, and then engage the gathered children in conversation or help them with a planned activity. This is a great opportunity to talk to the children, ask them questions, and to encourage them to listen to one another. For example:

> "Hi, welcome to this circle/table/class/etc. My name is [name], and I am glad you are here. While we wait for all of our friends to arrive, I wonder what happened this week that you are excited to share?"

The second adult leader sitting with the children now becomes the moderator as the group shares one at a time with one another. You might choose to have an opening activity the children can be doing while they engage in conversation and wait for the lesson to begin, or you might use this as a time to build community as the children practice listening and sharing with one another.

This is an unscripted time for you to get to know the children and for them to get to know you too. In these moments we model how to take turns, how to listen, and how to show that we respect one another. This is the first step in building community. This is also one of my favorite parts of teaching children. This is the time when I get to see and greet every child. It is also the time when I ask about their week, and listen as they share their stories from the days past. It can be a very rewarding and joy-filled time.

It is important that we also include in the liturgy or curriculum enough time for the children to get their bodies ready. This can be done with songs, games, chants, or body prayers. Any of these activities can help children get their wiggles out as they gather and prepare their hearts and minds for your time together. Follow a kinesthetic activity with a calming chant, song, or prayer as you invite the children to join you in the day's work.

MAINTAINING A SAFE SPACE

While the curriculum gives us guidance and tools regarding the intended lesson and learning objective of the day, much of our work in ministry with children is about inviting, encouraging, and guiding them as they learn how to live in Christian community with one another. In this space we practice the faith together, we learn from one another, and we support one another.

Honor the gift of *Kairos* time. In Greek, this word refers to the right, critical, or opportune moment. Often in the church we refer to *Kairos* time as God's time. In these moments when we embrace the opportunity God has given us, we remember and claim that we have all the time that we need. It is our adult tendency to rush through a well thought out and planned schedule. This is not the goal when sitting with children. While children need a structure (liturgy) to move through, remember the call to follow the flow of the liturgy together. Remember, the call is to dance. This requires a fluidity, a give and take, and a flexibility, even when the moves are choreographed. In this dance, we can take all the time we need to be present, to listen, and to faithfully respond. This requires flexibility and a deep grounding that allows us to breathe when the room feels chaotic and to rest assured that God's work is done even when we do not complete the curriculum exactly as it is prescribed.

Provide a group covenant, or a way of living together for the community when gathered. These expectations are set so that all people can be in community together. Every person, no matter their age, needs structure, boundaries, and a clear sense of expectations. Those expectations include behaviors. For example, you might remind children that "we listen when our friends are talking," or "we use kind words to help our friends know we care." You can invite the children to help you draft these best practices by creating a group covenant in which you all identify and accept the ways you will show up in community together. It is important to pay attention to cultural differences and expectations too. For example, some cultures expect eye contact where as other cultures see eye contact as intimidating, aggressive, and/or disrespectful. This is why it is important to have the entire community work on the covenant together.

When the children understand the expectations, they are much more willing to cooperate—and also to remind us of the rules! One very snowy and cold day, the room was full of children and adults with lots of pent up energy. Children were zooming around the room as I was patiently waiting for them to join me on the floor in our circle. One child observed what must have looked like chaos and stated: "Pastor Tanya, I think it is time to review the rules!" I smiled and said: "I completely agree." When we are clear in our expectations, when we invite the group to create a covenant together, when we pay attention to cultural expectations, and when we model best practices we can respond to times of chaos by reviewing the promises we have made together. This is work we do with grace and care, not with a legalistic and demanding attitude. Cultural awareness and respect for the children as individuals is essential. In response to a child who is yelling or talking over the group, you might say: "I know you know how to talk a little quieter. Can you show me how?" or "It's time to listen to our friends. Then when it is your time to talk, they will listen to you." When we model best practices, we encourage children and adults to practice skills reflected in their culture as crucial for community living. It is through such practice that children learn how to listen, share, and trust that their peers and the adults present will respect and honor what they say. This is the key to authentic conversation. It is up to us as the adults to guide these conversations making sure each person is honored, valued, and respected in the faith community.

Finally, if ministry has taught me anything, it is to be flexible. A child's needs change from day to day. One day a child may be able to get ready quickly, other days they may have difficulty getting ready and thus they need our patience, understanding, and time as they settle into their bodies. For this reason, it is well for us teachers to remain flexible as we move through the liturgy, knowing that on some days the gathering might take longer than others, and that on other days the prayer time or wondering time might need more time. Remember, the primary goal is not to finish the lesson plan but for each person to feel affirmed, experience God's presence and love, and leave with a deeper sense of relationship with God and neighbor through having been together. It is when this deep sense of security, trust, and acceptance are felt that children and adults blossom and their hearts and minds open to all the possibilities God presents in a given lesson or intentional time together.

When we set up this space well, holy conversation and faith formation will occur. Children will hear and claim what God is saying to them and to others, and they will discover ways to respond.

When we create a safe space built on trust and respect, children are more likely to engage in holy conversation with you and with one another. Children can easily tell if they have an adult's attention, and if that adult truly cares about what they are saying. When we set the stage well, children believe us when we say, "I wonder what you think," and they respond openly and freely. This opens the door for the holy work of wondering and listening to God and each other.

Two tools that help us connect to God and neighbor as we discern how God is calling us to respond are to practice active wondering and to practice active listening.

PRACTICING ACTIVE WONDERING

Active wondering creates space for authentic and honest conversation. Such wondering begins with the understanding that there may be more than one answer to a given question. By asking open-ended questions, we open our minds to all of the possibilities that a question holds and ignite curiosity in the conversation participants. "I wonder" questions present an invitation into holy conversation. They create a space for children to share freely, to address issues of power and authority, and to nurture honest and raw conversation and feedback. Using this method in a safe space built on trust and respect frees children to contribute their thoughts willingly, decreasing the risk of providing an expected answer or parroting another adult figure in their community. Active wondering nurtures and fuels a continued dialogue, encouraging participants to share their own reflections and insights. This creates space for all of the theologians in the room to join in the divine dance as they discern what God is saying to them in that moment, and as they share that insight with the entire group.

Wondering with children can have significant impact in ministry settings. "Children need to learn how to wonder in religious education so they can 'enter' religious language rather than merely repeat it or talk about it."[8] Through modeling, the teacher encourages this process, giving permission for all present to wonder out loud, inviting both the children and the adults to participate in the conversation by sharing new insight and discoveries. Some examples of wondering questions from *Godly Play* and my research liturgy include:

- I wonder how you felt God's presence this week?
- I wonder what is your favorite part of the story?
- I wonder how you discovered yourself in this story?
- I wonder how you experienced God in this story?
- I wonder if there's any part of the story we can leave out and still have all the story we need?
- I wonder what you wonder about?

Teachers do this work as shepherds. Shepherds guide the conversation and model helpful language as the community explores its religious language and understanding. Elizabeth Caldwell in her book, *I Wonder: Engaging a Child's Curiosity about the Bible*, argues that we can help children learn a faith vocabulary by "opening space in busy lives."[9] We create space to do this work and then, as shepherds, we ask the big questions and invite participants to respond. We might participate in the conversation too, however it is essential that as the shepherd and guide we avoid being the first and the last person to share. Instead, we can open the conversation with a wondering question: "I wonder how you experienced God this week," then we can insert our wonderings after some of the children have had a chance to respond, followed by an invitation for the children to join in again too. It is important that we facilitate mutual conversation that is not overwhelmed by the voices of adults. When the time comes to close the conversation simply conclude with an affirming statement: "Thank you for wondering with me today"—rather than ending with one final contribution. Refraining from oversharing or learning to sit in silence are often the hardest parts of this pedagogical approach. As shepherds and guides, our task is to learn how to be comfortable with silence as we wait for a participant to share. When I begin this work with a new group, I find it often takes a couple of sessions for participants to trust that the space is

8. Berryman, *Godly Play*, 60.
9. Caldwell, *I Wonder*, loc. 1051.

safe enough to wonder out loud (rather than be clever or give the "right" answer). Building a safe space where participants feel brave enough to share takes time and intentional work.

Thankfully, as shepherds we can be a non-anxious presence in the silence knowing that God is at work as the participants wonder silently and process their experience in that moment. At the end of the silence, the shepherd might choose to ask another question, or if the time for conversation has ended, say: "Sometimes we do our best work in our hearts and in our heads. When you are ready, I hope you will share your wonderings with me and others." Over time children will begin to trust the space (and you) and begin to open up, sharing their theological wonderings and reflections. Our work is to encourage and patiently wait for each person to be ready to share.

Nurturing this space and creating an environment where children want to share requires a deep sense of trust of all participants in the leadership, the members of the community, and the process. Leaders must model and maintain a safe space where all wonderings are heard and considered. While some responses might be particularly humorous or fitting, it is important that children and adults alike honor every answer that is presented, and that they not respond simply with an affirmation to the wondering, such as "I really like that answer" but instead use every response as an opportunity to further the conversation. For example: "Hmmm, thank you for sharing. I wonder what others think?"

It is through active wondering, beginning each question with "I wonder," that we teachers and guides invite and encourage children to share their stories, reminding them that their thoughts matter, that they have something to teach us and the rest of the community. As one eight-year-old boy stated in one of my research sessions, "Wonder is a good word." Wonder is indeed a good word and an important tool for ministry with children. Wonder is an active word that invites us to participate without judgment, to create without seeking perfection, and to try without the fear of being corrected or being presented with the "correct" answer. Our role as adults in ministry with children is not to provide children with information or the correct answer.

Indeed, this type of banking pedagogy and simple answers to big questions actually shut down conversation and prohibit learning.

> Young children are quite comfortable with mystery, with inconclusiveness. They know that much of life is incomprehensible and

therefore mysterious. Older children might find it helpful to know that there are not always clear cut answers to everything, and that to pretend that there are displaces or even represses the true mysteriousness of existence.[10]

We can encourage children in the work of reflection, wondering, and discovery by inviting them into the mystery and into the realm of possibilities.

Active wondering can be an invitation to conversation and discovery. This takes practice. Recall, first, that our work is not to provide answers, but to hold the space open, to invite wonder and awe, and to encourage possibilities and discovery. Recall, second, that we must choose our responses carefully. Our options during an active wondering session are to respond with:

- Silence: Silence creates space for all participants to take in what has been said and added to the conversation. Often another participant will respond when we give silent time and space for contemplation.
- Encouragement: We encourage what is said by noting, "Thank you for sharing," or "I wonder about that too."
- Clarification: We can use the opportunity to clarify what we hear the participant saying by repeating what the child said ("Hmmm, God is with us when we are scared") or by saying, "That's interesting. Can you tell me more about that?"
- Another Wondering Question: Follow up with another wondering question like, "Thank you for all your thoughts. I wonder what God is calling us to do next?"

The following example of a wondering session comes out of my research project, where I wondered with a young child during the individual art response time in which I invited the children to reflect on the lesson for that day:

Teacher: "John,[11] I wonder what you are creating?"

John: "I'm working on a man, driving a farm truck, like he's trying to get home."

Teacher: "I wonder how that reminds you of God?"

---

10. Hay and Nye, *Spirit of the Child*, 72.
11. Name changed for anonymity.

> John: "Maybe God tried to help him find his way home."
>
> Teacher: "I wonder why God helped him find his way home?"
>
> John: "When something bad happens, God can help him."
>
> Teacher: "Hmmm, I wonder how that feels?"
>
> John: "It is good to know God helps us."
>
> Teacher: "It *is* good to know God helps us. Thank you for sharing with me to today."

When we work to create safe space and encourage others to wonder what God is saying to them that day, participants of all ages respond. When we invite and encourage them to wonder, children willingly respond to the questions and begin asking questions of their own.

Watching children and adults wonder sparks joy as all participants open their hearts and minds to every possibility God provides.

> Children begin to respond to the wondering with their eyes and their bodies. They lean in. Their eyes sparkle. Some carry on an inner dialogue without words; others play with words within their own silent conversation. Others speak out loud.[12]

In this process we open ourselves to discover something new. Even as adults we have much to learn and discover. As Berryman explains in *Godly Play*:

> Think how many times I've worked with the Parable of the Mustard Seed. Who knows how many times? I still love the parable, and there are still new things waiting for me whenever I go into it again to see . . . there is always something new to be found there if we have the eyes to see and the ears to hear.[13]

When we join with the children in this wondering process, we open our hearts and minds to all the possibilities God presents. We offer an invitation for people of all ages to participate in God's dance as we listen for God and discern what God is saying to us and our community on that day.

It is through this process that we model and practice theological reflection, sharing our insight with others. This tool creates space for us to do holy work together. When I asked the children at the end of my research project what their favorite part of our time together was, several children

---

12. Hay and Nye, *Spirit of the Child*, 35.
13. Berryman, *Godly Play*, 35.

responded: "It was the question marks." I used the symbol of question marks to describe our times of wondering together. I responded to their reflection by saying: "That was one of my favorite parts too. Thank you for wondering with me."

PRACTICING ACTIVE LISTENING

The second tool that helps us connect to God and neighbor is active listening. Of course active wondering and listening go hand and hand. Wondering opens space for adults to engage in active listening, and vice versa. When we are authentic in our wonderings we are much more likely to listen well to the responses that we invite, and our listening then leads to more questions. I often find that real and authentic conversation leaves me with more questions than answers, and yet through holy conversation I feel closer to God and neighbor and hear clearly what God is calling me to do next.

Active listening is a gift that we can offer people of all ages in our communities. Children are often looked over, shushed, or ignored. The gift of listening enables us to affirm a child's presence, to acknowledge their feelings, and to encourage their wonderings. Those of us who commit our lives to ministry with children understand deeply the wisdom and joy they bring to our lives. When we open space for active listening and authentic conversation, we create an opportunity for all to experience God's presence amongst us. Fred Rogers is one who deeply understood the importance of listening and actively created space to join in holy conversation with children. He understood listening as an essential part of any conversation. Rogers helped us see how it is through listening that we grow to understand and love our neighbor. "Questions are such a powerful way to say, 'I care about what you have to say, and I want to know more about you.'"[14] Rather than trying to teach children through entertainment and amusement, Mr. Rogers reminds us that "We don't need silly hats or cheap tricks to engage children. We need only be there to listen and give their brains the opportunity to develop through sensory exploration."[15]

Therefore, active listening begins with being authentically present. We adults in ministry with children do well to enter into any conversation with a willingness to learn and a desire to understand the persons with

---

14. Sharapan, "What We Can Learn," 2.
15. Neville, *Won't You Be My Neighbor?*

whom we are in ministry. This is a gift we can give as we create space for holy conversation.

Through this gift of active listening we create space for all persons to recognize and claim God's active presence in our lives. In the *Godly Play* story of Abraham, *The Great Family*, we hear the storyteller say: "Then God came so close to Abram, and Abram came so close to God, that [Abram] knew what God wanted him to do."[16] Many children who hear this story often identify this as their favorite part. As they share how they like it when Abraham knew what God was saying, we take time to have conversation about the importance of listening to God and to each other. Listening, children tell me, is when we get to share our stories, when we get to know each other better. This is indeed holy work. Through active listening, we are not only giving children space to reflect and discern, we are also modeling how they might offer this gift to others. When we join in holy conversation and truly listen to one another, we create space for connecting to God and to our neighbors. It is in these holy moments that God speaks, and when we are paying attention we know what God is saying.

Active listening invites children into the conversation, encouraging them in their discernment. When we show up authentically and intentionally create safe space, there is room for this holy work to begin. We begin as mentioned above using the tool of active wondering, asking a big question and giving space for the group to ponder the question. We then offer the gift of silence. This is often hard for children and for adults who have not practiced this tool. Silence is a religious language that needs to be modeled and practiced. It is in silence that we are able to open ourselves to the movement of the spirit. As we turn off the worldly chatter, we can begin to hear more clearly what God is saying to us in that moment.

Silence as religious language is a gift children and adults can share with one another. We share this gift by showing and modeling it for each other. When we do not create space for silence, we close off authentic conversation, and in doing so "the mutual learning between children and adults breaks down."[17]

Modeling and practicing silence can be hard work for people of all ages. This is why it is essential that we provide opportunities to practice together in these sacred spaces. Therefore, in our authentic presence, we must invite and welcome silence as participants take time for internal processing

---

16. Berryman, *Complete Guide to Godly Play*, 2:90.
17. Berryman, "Silence is Stranger," 264.

and reflection. This looks different across ministry settings. We adults model this work when we ask a wondering question, then sit back and patiently wait for children to respond. Some children may respond more quickly than their peers. Other children might be uncomfortable with this practice and so they might respond by fidgeting or wiggling. Some might welcome the practice and refrain from speaking. All of these responses are welcomed as we practice silence together. We can thank them for their hard work, affirm that we can see how they are all thinking, and state that we look forward to hearing what they are wondering about.

When the silence is broken, it is important that we adults do not rush to respond. We might have initial thoughts in response to what the child shared. We might rush to judge whether their comment is right or wrong in our eyes. But in these moments we must set aside our preconceived notions and hidden agendas and listen to the child and hear what they might be saying to us. As the children share their reflections, they give us the space to consider: "What do I hear? What wisdom, gifts, or theological insight are revealed in this statement?" Honor what the children and other participants already know. Children are very aware of their relationships and the reality of the world around them. Honor their experience by asking them to share what they know or are concerned about. As children share, you continue to invite them to participate in the dance of wondering, listening, and sharing. As participants share their wonderings you can encourage their wondering saying, "Thank you for sharing. What I hear you saying is . . ." then sit back and wait for the child to respond. You can then follow up and say to the group, "I wonder what you all are wondering?" If/when someone interrupts another person, remind the interrupter that "[Name] is speaking. Let's listen to them. I know that you would want us to listen to you. You will have a chance to share. Thank you for listening." This is a dance that takes time for a community to learn together. We all learn by participating in this dance together. By modeling and encouraging each participant to listen to the other, we are practicing this holy work together and sharpening this spiritual tool.

CONCLUSION

God calls us to create safe spaces for holy conversation with the children with whom we are in ministry. Through these intentional and authentic conversations, children and adults find space to listen to God and to discern how they might respond to all they are hearing and experiencing. We participate in the divine dance of wondering and listening together as we consider: "What is God saying to us today?" It is in this space that we recognize and claim God's presence in our lives. Our call to ministry with children requires these holy conversations as we support each other in the process of faith formation.

As the young boy taught me those many years ago, holy conversations create space for us to see and hear one another, to wrestle with our deep questions of the faith, and to discover ways to respond together. One of my professors stated in response to my research project, "What you have taught me is that if we are not paying attention and listening to children . . . it is not that we are missing an opportunity to teach them . . . but we run the risk of missing God at work in our communities and our world."

When we create safe spaces where we can wonder and listen together, we are indeed engaging in holy work, learning and growing together. It is through this process that we encourage and model for children how to do the work of meaning making—not by giving them information, but by inviting them and guiding them, by sharing stories and asking questions, by inviting them to share stories and ask questions and by listening to what they say. We will take a deeper look at how to do this in Chapter 4.

chapter 4

HOLY CONVERSATIONS WITH GOD

"I wonder is a good word." —Anonymous (age 8)

Children are theologians, continually making meaning in response to their daily experiences through holy conversations with God, one another, and the adults who journey alongside them. This is their theological work. This chapter examines how children do this theological work of making meaning of the Divine's presence in their lives. It uses stories from experience and research to illustrate how the children's reflections, insights, and wonderings help them make meaning as they discover ways to respond to God's grace and love.

CHILD'S HERMENEUTICAL LENS

Young children make meaning through their own experiences, which means primarily through the people, places, and objects familiar to them. In this rather literal stage of life, children tend to parrot the words and opinions of others in their community. What they experience themselves and what they hear from others become the lenses through which they see, and the ears and mind through which they process their experiences.

We see this parroting, this assumption of others' worldviews, in moments like the children's time in the worship service where they have limited time for wondering and reflection. For many churches this is a short, five-minute gathering in which an adult shares a story and sometimes asks children questions prompted by the story. Since in such contexts there is not enough time to create a safe space for wondering and reflection, children often respond rather automatically to these questions with "Jesus," having learned from the community's teachings that this is indeed often the answer.

As we work to create more space for wonderings and discovery, we might find that the children with whom we work start from this very literal worldview. If their answers seem simplistic, it is because they are just beginning the hard work of making meaning and processing life theologically. Our work as shepherds and guides is to honor this process, meeting children where they are at, acknowledging their reflections, and encouraging their wonderings. This is true even if we think they are simply repeating/parroting another adult in their lives, or if we believe they are just giving an answer they think others will accept—a.k.a. "Jesus." Indeed: they are "trying out language" as they consider what they are experiencing and find words to describe their thoughts and feeling.

The work of faith formation leaders is to create a space where children can show up authentically and wonder freely, space where they can discover and develop their own religious language and understandings. In the beginning, most of the children with whom I worked revealed their logical and literal processing skills anytime I asked them a question. They repeated what others in the room had just said, or they would tell me what another important person in their lives had told them. For example, on the first day I asked the wondering question: "I wonder where God is in this story?" and a child responded, "My mom says God is always with us." To encourage this young person in this work, I followed up with another question: "Hmmm, God is always with us . . . I wonder what that feels like?" Immediately the children started expressing different emotions: "Good, happy, safe . . ." and the list continued as the children continued to add adjectives to the conversation. Though children often start from the literal space, where they repeat what they have seen or heard, with time and practice they begin to uncover their own understandings and they develop their own religious language for describing what they know to be true. Thankfully, children are eager to participate in this meaning-making process.

PARTICIPATORY ACTION RESEARCH: LEARNING FROM THE CHILDREN

In order to understand how children make meaning, I needed to spend time listening to and learning from children. As a qualitative researcher

I wanted to find a way to engage in Participatory Action Research (PAR) with the children. The goal of PAR is to create a research environment where there is:

> (a) a collective commitment to investigate an issue or problem, (b) a desire to engage in self—and collective reflection to gain clarity about the issue under investigation, (c) a joint decision to engage in individual and/or collective action that leads to a useful solution that benefits the people involved, and (d) the building of alliances between researchers and participants in the planning, implementation, and dissemination of the research process.[1]

This method achieves these aims through a "cyclical process of exploration, knowledge construction, and action at different moments throughout the research process."[2] "PAR is distinct in its focus on collaboration, political engagement, and an explicit commitment to social justice."[3]

I delighted in working alongside the children in this participatory process, learning from the feedback, insight, and direction they gave me along the way.[4] Their wisdom helped shape the process and the outcome of our time together.

As a final step to this process, I presented my findings to the children after reviewing and analyzing all the data. I wanted to give every child space to continue to form the research findings of this study, and to ensure that I was understanding their journey correctly. In reviewing and analyzing the data, and in preparing to present my findings to the children, I spent an enormous amount of time in prayer trying to discern how to present the material in a way that would invite and encourage the children to participate fully, to share faithfully, and to comment honestly.

Recognizing that every session I spent with the children included a time of story using objects and materials that the children could physically touch and engage with, I wanted to share the research data in a similar form. After many failed ideas, I reviewed the video transcripts one more time and suddenly was reminded of a young participant who enjoyed putting together puzzles. She would go to work, diligently picking up the pieces, turning them around, trying them out next to all of the possibilities, before

---

1. McIntyre, *Participatory Action Research*, 1.
2. McIntyre, *Participatory Action Research*, 1.
3. Denzin and Lincoln, *Sage Handbook*, 388.
4. An important step in my research was the consent process where I made sure to have the consent of each church, all the parents/guardians, and the children too.

snapping a puzzle piece into place. After placing two pieces together, this young child would sit back on her heels and review the picture. When she seemed content with her decision, she surveyed the remaining pieces, and resumed the process with another piece. I thought of this young girl often as I watched video after video of recorded sessions from my time with these children. I pictured her considering every puzzle piece as I sifted through and reviewed the children's artwork as well as the pictures they took every week for their photo journal of how they experienced God.

One afternoon I was thinking about this puzzle-making process as I was reading the transcripts of one of the very first sessions in which I'd explained the research process to the children. One perspicacious young person had suggested: "So we are helping you with your homework?" "Yes," I replied. "You are helping me with my work, and I'm hoping we will discover answers together." Another young person jumped in: "Do you have a hypothesis?" "I do have a hypothesis," I stated. "But I don't want to share that with you just yet. I want to see what you all teach me without me providing any information that might disrupt the process." I then told him that at the end of our time together I would share with them my hypothesis and conclusions and give them a chance to respond.

Three months later, as I sat analyzing the data and considering my pedagogical response, I realized that all along we had been picking up the pieces, considering each moment, and trying to decide how they all fit into the larger puzzle.

It became clear that the pieces to the children's meaning-making process are: Engage, Recognize, Claim, and Respond—to God's grace and love in the world. As the children engage, recognize, claim, and respond to God's presence in their lives, they participate in the holy dance, growing closer to God and making a difference in their home, community, and the world.

ENGAGE

The first puzzle piece in the children's theological method is when they *engage* or connect to God and each other. It is the moment or moments when children open their hearts and minds, connect to the Holy, and consider all of the possibilities their experiences and the dance provides.

One day, as I began the day's story, I noticed one child who kept shifting around in his spot in the circle. First, he shifted from side to side. Then he put his hands in his lap; lay down, his fist tucked under his chin; and finally sighed audibly as he swung out his legs and leaned back. Raising his hand, he asked: "Pastor Tanya, can I lie down? I just can't seem to get my body ready to listen today."

I agreed that getting ready is sometimes hard work, and invited him to lie down if that would help him experience the story. (My only stipulation was that he needed to keep his arms and legs in his own space to ensure he was not distracting his friend). He quickly lay down, his hand under his chin, and settled into this posture. As I began the story I could see a physical shift in his body posture and facial expression. It was as if a weight had lifted from his shoulders and he was able to relax into the process.

It is hard to describe in words the physical shifts I see on the video of this moment, yet we all know that when we pay attention we can see children physically and audibly lock into the process. I call it the moment of engagement. They may not be sitting completely still, but they are truly experiencing all that is taking place. There was one child there who continually spun around, stopping every few minutes to see what was happening in the middle of the circle as the story unfolded. Was she even paying attention? As I told the story of Abraham and Sarah taking a long journey to their new home, and as I described how Abraham stopped to pray, I could see her eyes locking in on the manipulatives every so often as the story introduced a new location or a new action.

Following the story, I gave the children an opportunity to process the story through various response options. This is their work. I noticed the young girl who continued to spin during the story working with LEGO bricks. At the end of the work time I asked her: "Would you like to tell me about your work?" She looked up at me and then back at the LEGO brick creation, and then back at me as if to say: "You can't tell?" I waited a few more seconds and then she sighed and said: "It's the story! I built Abraham's and Sarah's journey!" She then proceeded to retell the story by walking me through her LEGO creation, stopping at the places where "Abraham talked to God and Abraham knew what God was saying." "I really liked this part," she stated. I was taken completely by surprise. I thought that she was not paying attention, and yet she had clearly heard and remembered the whole story. When I went back to watch the video later, despite her movement, it was clear that she was engaged with the story. Her eye movement and eye contact gave it away. When I paid attention, I could clearly see her engaging.

When we adults pay attention, we can see and hear children engaging with the world around them. Their body language reveals their interest, focus, and curiosity. Nothing revealed this to me as a researcher more than the video from the day when I forgot to turn on the microphone. I had sixty minutes of data without sound and yet I decided to analyze it. I observed the children's body language as they engaged in their work that day. I saw interactions with others, I saw furrowed brows as they watched the story unfold, I witnessed children's eagerness as they excitedly raised their hands ready to share. Each of these moments helped me understand that we engage with the world around us and with our creator with our entire bodies. This is an important piece of the meaning-making process.

When we believe God to be moving in and through creation, then we can begin to recognize how God is in the midst of these moments. Children, therefore, can engage with God and each other throughout the day and over their lifetime. As they pay attention to the world around them, children take in the sights and sounds, gathering information that helps them make meaning of everything and everyone they encounter. This is true of the Divine too. When children are invited and encouraged to engage with the Holy, children pay attention and participate. As they process such experiences, they develop their own language and understanding. Our work as adults is therefore to create space for children to connect with God and to invite the children to experience the Bible. In this safe and welcoming space children do the holy work of engaging with God and each other, making meaning and growing in their faith.

RECOGNIZE

To recognize is to identify someone or something from having encountered them before; it is to know again.[5] As children engage and pay attention to God and their community, they begin to recognize the Holy's presence in multiple facets of their lives. They encounter God again as they remember and identify moments when they experienced God in other moments of their lives. Recognition is the second piece in the child's meaning-making puzzle.

One afternoon, as I concluded the day's story and began wondering aloud with the children, one child exclaimed: "God is everywhere!" Another piped up: "It is like God is reaching his hands out, offering the world

---

5. Oxford Languages, "Recognize."

a hug. God's love is with everyone." Another child shared, "God is sitting right here next to me." A third child recognized that "God is with me when I am scared." And another stated: "God is with me when I am lost and alone." Each of these exclamations points to the children's ability to recognize God in the midst of their experiences. One child shared a story of when he was lost in the mall. He said that as he waited for his parents to find him, he talked to God, and he knew God was with him. Another young person said that when she is happy she knows God is with her. Whether in children's joy, fear, or sadness, God is present. Children recognize this presence when they are invited to pay attention to it and to share.

Catholic theologian Karl Rahner argues that from the beginning, children are partners of God, aware of the divine transcendence.[6] There is a "direct relationship to God which is achieved at each of the stages in human development and growth, and so in childhood too."[7] Children possess gifts that help them engage in a faithful relationship with the Holy. "All human beings—including children—have capacity in human freedom to experience the divine self-communication."[8] Claiming that children are deeply and intrinsically connected to the Holy, and knowing that children have the gifts they need to access the Divine, affirms the child's ability to recognize, to identify, and to know God when they experience God in their daily lives. Theologian Catherine LaCugna suggests that "we should think of God existing concretely as persons in communion with other persons."[9] For faith formation is relational. We meet God when we interact with others. God reveals Godself in our interactions with humanity and creation. Children are capable of recognizing God in their interactions and experiences. This is an important piece of their meaning making as they identify the Holy's presence in their lives.

We might have a difficult time proving God's existence, but when we pay attention we catch a glimpse of the Holy at work in the world. One child shared a story of sitting on a swing at her grandmother's farm looking out at the land, feeling the wind blow, and knowing that God was with her. To recognize is not the same as understanding fully. To recognize is not a scientific moment in which the invisible God becomes visible, measurable, and precise. Sometimes we cannot even fully articulate or describe what

---

6. Rahner, "Ideas for a Theology of Childhood," 38.
7. Rahner, "Ideas for a Theology of Childhood," 33.
8. Mercer, *Welcoming Children*, 150.
9. LaCugna, *God for Us*, 225.

it is we have experienced. Instead, these moments of recognition become significant memories of when we or a child experiences anew the mysterious presence of God. It is in these moments that "the life of God is made concrete, [that] God touches the creature through self-communicating love, [that] God exists as God for us."[10] In these moments, children seem to recognize the promise that is foundational to the doctrine of prevenient grace—that from the very beginning God is with us. It may not be a concrete understanding but it is a moment when heart and mind are opened to this wondrous possibility. The times when they recognized God's presence become the foundational building blocks of their faith and their continuing relationship with the Divine. When we recognize, we know for a brief moment. When we note or remember these moments, we are helping children lay down bread crumbs to which they can return later in life. Our hope is that one day the aforementioned girl might say: "I remember when I experienced God at my grandmother's farm. I want to go back to that place, to the time when I knew God was with me." It is our adult work to help children recognize God and build these faith memories that help them connect to God and identify ways to return to those moments of certainty when life does not feel so certain or trustworthy.

As mentioned in Chapter 3, the *Godly Play* story, *The Great Family*, describes the journey of Abraham and Sarah.[11] As Abraham leads his family to the next stop in the journey, he takes time to build an altar, and to talk to God. In these moments "God comes so close to Abraham and Abraham comes so close to God that Abraham knew what God was saying." These moments are the story's way of documenting when Abraham recognized God's presence.

When I told this story, many of the children shared that their favorite part was when Abraham talked to God. They would point to the altars built with rocks and remember how God came so close to Abraham and Abraham came so close to God. One child called these moments "stampers." "They're stampers," he stated, pointing to the pile of rocks marking or stamping the places were Abraham prayed. "They help us remember where Abraham talked to God." Stampers are essential for each of us as we develop a deep relationship with God. They help us remember where, when, and how we experienced God and they give us a place to which to return when we feel lost and alone.

10. LaCugna, *God for Us*, 410.
11. Berryman, *Complete Guide to Godly Play*, 2:85–94.

In these moments of recognition, we see how the "occasion is touched by God and how children gain "knowledge of God drawn from experience."[12] Often described as "God moments" by those who work with children and youth, these experiences are the child's "witness to the nature of God through the creative mark of God in the world, like footprints not yet erased from the sand."[13] As children listen to, wonder at, and process their lives, they join the dance of faith and begin to recognize God's presence in their experiences.

We witness these moments of recognition in the children's descriptions of God, in their prayers, and in their art. They are often "aha" moments—moments of surprise or of confirmation. They might be hard to pinpoint, and if we are not careful, we can miss them, and so can the children. Such moments of recognition of the Holy are often revealed in a facial expression, a wondering, an emotion, or a feeling, but also in children's drawings and other art in which they note God's presence in the world. Children often describe these moments as experiences of beauty, love, joy, and hope. They mark that there is something beyond what we can sense, something within and yet beyond the material world.

The child's work, then, is to pay attention and testify to the moments when they feel God's presence. Such attention and such testimonies are an essential part of the child's theological process, of marking important moments on their faith journey and as they strive to remember "God with them." Children's recognition of God in their midst is a gateway to deeper wondering and consequential awareness that supports and fuels their continued faith development.

Our adult work is to support the child's work by wondering with them about their faith experiences. We can ask them: "I wonder how you experience God?" and invite them to share and "stamp" their faith moments. Our work is to create space for these moments, encouraging children to pay attention. And then, when the children participate and share, our job is to help children capture these moments too.

CLAIM

As children engage and recognize the Holy in their lives, they begin to claim this presence, practicing religious language that helps them mark

12. Suchocki, *God, Christ, Church*, 39.
13. Suchocki, *God, Christ, Church*, 41.

their experiences with God. The process of claiming God's presence in their lives is the third piece in the children's theological method. As children recognize the Holy's presence in their lives, they begin to claim this presence by sharing and remembering how, when, and where they experienced God. This narrative, whether spoken, drawn, prayed, or otherwise shared, becomes the memory marker that ground children in their faith, the experiences in life to which they return.

One of my favorite aspects of my time with children is when I ask them, "How did you experience God this week?" Every child shares their own experience. While it takes time to create a space in which it feels safe enough to share something so intimate, after two to three weeks together children were eager to share their memory markers, their experiences. One morning, a seven-year-old girl shared with the group: "I experienced God this morning in worship. When I sit in the sanctuary and my grandmother plays the organ, I can feel God is with me. Today as I listened to my grandmother play, I looked at all the stained-glass windows and took time to talk to God."

I end every session by saying, "Don't forget to pay attention this week to how you experience God. I can't wait to hear all about it when we are together again." This call to pay attention—or this "homework" as some of the kids call it—is a reminder and an invitation for all in the room to keep their hearts, eyes, ears, and minds open this new week, paying attention and expecting God at every turn.

The more children claim God in their lives, the more they practice and develop religious language that helps them describe and remember their experience. In response to my weekly opening question, the children often begin their narratives with "I experienced God when . . ." Our younger and still more literal children often link God's presence to a specific time and/or place, using these as ways to describe and put words to their experience. They do this work from the very beginning of their lives, when they are an infant practicing sounds to when they are an older child trying to find words to describe what they are experiencing.

Children develop internally and externally. Language gives them a means to express what they are processing internally, and to share their thoughts with the broader world. Psychologist Lev Vygotsky, argues that the internal process "starts from the whole, from the meaningful complex, and only later begins to master the separate semantic units," or the various parts of their experience.[14] For example, young children may see a landscape covered in white and feel cold. This is the whole experience. This is what children take in and begin to process internally. Over time, children will be able to distinguish the parts of that landscape. They will recognize the buildings, the tree, the branches, and the missing leaves, all covered in a wet layer of something people call snow. Moving from whole to part internally, children develop the ability to respond to an experience, isolating and distinguishing the individual parts and making associations in response to their developed understanding of that experience. Snow becomes associated with cold. A mother's arms that are used to hug become associated with safety and love. A whole experience of pain, isolation, or shame leads to the child associating that space, person, or individual objects of that whole experience with fear. The whole experience creates an inner narrative that then impacts how a person associates themselves with the various parts of that experience. Vygotsky argues that these memories and reflections on experience become "one of the central psychological functions upon which all the other functions are built . . . for the very young child to think means to remember."[15]

The external plane of development is the reverse. As children begin to verbally articulate their experiences their narratives come at first with short one word responses and as their language develops they find ways to articulate the whole experience in all of its complexities and nuances. Over time, the development of language gives them a means to verbalize what they are processing internally, to share their thoughts with the outer world. The development of language, Vygotsky suggest, begins with an articulation of part of the experience as children have limited word choices in their early stages of development. Over time, they move from externally processing part of the experience to sharing the whole experience as they learn new words that help describe their experiences. One of my son's first words was "hot." This came in response to his introduction to table foods. Often, when we sat down for dinner, our son would reach out for the food on the table. My husband and I would quickly respond, "that's hot, we need to wait a minute." Over time our son quickly started externally pointing to food and declaring: "hot." More recently he now has begun asking it with a different inflection as if to ask "hot?" As we respond, "yes, that is hot, let's wait . . ." or "no, it is not hot, you can try it . . ." I recognize that we

14. Vygotsky, *Thought and Language*, 219.
15. Vygotsky, *Mind in Society*, 50.

are modeling language as he continues to develop moving from being able to articulate part of the experience to verbalizing his whole experience. One day I imagine he will say: "That food is hot, I think I'll wait." Until then, "hot" helps him make meaning and share his understanding as he engages with the world around him.

As children begin to find words to articulate and describe their whole experience, they develop language for sharing that experience with others. Language gives them a means to express what they are processing internally, to share their thoughts with the outer world. The development of religious language then gives children the ability to express and share their experiences of God with others. Learning religious language, "is like learning any art . . . you have to use it to know it and the earlier you begin to know it, the easier it is to become fluent."[16] This is how children move from *recognizing* God's love—experiencing the large picture—to *claiming* God's love—practicing language that gives them the ability to express all of the many parts of their experiences and learnings.

Claiming God's presence and love is the act of remembering these important moments in our lives. Just as Vygotsky pairs thinking with remembering, when children process and claim their experiences, they begin to make meaning that they will remember as they respond to God's presence in their lives. The young child listening to her grandmother play the organ told me, "When I listen to the music I know God is with me." In this moment the child begins to process and make meaning out of her experiences. Music potentially becomes a reminder of God's presence and love. Piaget asserts that as children develop language, they begin to make connections in response to what they hear and see. The process of meaning making occurs as the neurons within the brain fire in response to outside stimuli, fire, creating new connections within the neural system, and developing a biological awareness. This biological awareness, or memory, provides the body with information that can be accessed and used at a later date. Memory making then, is the way that the brain organizes the information it collects in response to a person's numerous experiences. These memories become the "stampers" that help children remember their experiences with God. They become the foundation to their faith, grounding each child in their own awareness and narrative of God's presence in their lives. I will say more about memory markers and stampers as tools children use to claim God's presence in Chapter 5.

---

16. Berryman, *Spiritual Guidance of Children*, loc. 165.

Claiming God's presence and finding words to describe these experiences is an important part of the meaning-making process. As children recognize God in their midst, they begin to vocalize and claim their experiences of God's presence and love. At times the recognition and claiming might seem intertwined, but by listening carefully one can witness a child not only recognizing God's presence (I felt God's love) but claiming this presence and its impact on or in their lives: "I know God loves me. I know God is with me. I am God's child, etc."

Now more than ever, it is essential that children do this important work of developing religious language that helps them claim God's presence and love in their lives. The world children live in is broken. The youngest members of our communities are experiencing hate, division, and inequality that is modeled for them in their daily lives, talked about by their community, and shared through digital platforms and the twenty-four hour news cycle. Our children are not immune to the realities of our world and they are greatly impacted by what they experience. After learning of the unjust deaths of black men and women via social media and the news children ask questions including: "Why are people so mean to one another?" "Why can't people be nice to each other?" "Why do people care if people look different?" "How can one be Christian and say mean things about others?" These are all very big questions. Practicing and developing religious language helps children begin to articulate and claim their own understanding in response to these questions. "God makes us unique and loves us all the same." "We are different and beautiful in the eyes of God." "God loves me and you!" As children claim their experiences of God's presence and love they develop religious language that helps them articulate the meaning made. Their theological wonderings then open space for them to share their wisdom and insight as they speak into a hurting world. Claiming God's presence and love in their lives and in the lives of others, children find ways to articulate and model their understanding of how God calls us to be in relationships with God and others.

Our work as adults who journey with children is to model religious language, and to encourage children as they develop and practice their own, in so doing remembering Mr. Rogers' wisdom, "Anything that is human is mentionable, and anything that is mentionable is manageable."[17] In modeling such language, we also create space in which children can share, develop, and practice their language together. It makes such language and such practice

17. Kris, "What's Mentionable Is Manageable."

normal. When we give voice to our sense of being loved by God, when we share our stories and our experiences, we support one another in faith formation and discipleship. "When we can talk about our feelings, they become less overwhelming, less upsetting, and less scary."[18] By claiming our own experiences of God, we affirm God's presence and we invite others to recognize God's presence in the world for themselves. This piece of the theological process is the outward confirmation of God's mysterious presence.

RESPOND

When we practice this work together, we not only affirm God's presence in our lives but we begin to hear how God wants us to respond. This is the fourth and final piece of the puzzle—the piece where children discern and discover how God is calling them to respond to all they have experienced. It is also in this space that children move from hearing to responding with faithful action, living into their faith as they respond to God's presence in their lives.

Whether children process this awareness of God's presence internally or externally, we can provide opportunities for children to reflect on the information they are taking in, to make connections, and to store their insights for future use. Through this meaning process, children begin to discern how to respond to all they are experiencing. For example, they do not stop at a simple narrative such as "God loves me" but instead continue the conversation: "God loves me, and I want to share that love with others."

Berryman's and Stewart's Story, *The Light*, is an impactful story for the children I have worked with.[19] This story gives children the opportunity to experience a candle being lit for every individual in the room. During the telling of this story, as the candle is extinguished or "the light is changed," the storyteller says, "the light that was once in one place is now in many places." Children watch in awe as the snuffer puts out the flame, the smoke fills the snuffer, and then proceeds to fill the room. In the wondering that follows the story, the storyteller asks, "I wonder what your favorite part of the story is?" Many children respond: "When I received my light." Later in the conversation, the storyteller asks: "I wonder what you wonder about?" In response, an eight-year-old boy responds: "I wonder how I can share my light with others." This same child really engaged with this story and chose

18. Kris, "What's Mentionable Is Manageable."
19. Stewart and Berryman, *Young Children*, 71–77.

to retell this story every week as his "work." He would take time (with the research assistant's help) lighting each candle, making sure he lit a candle for every child in the room, and then at the end of the work session he would ask the research assistant if he could "change everyone's light so their lights could be in many places at many times." One week he came to me and said: "I know what my work is!" I responded: "Do you want to work with the story of the light again?" This child responded: "No . . . my real work." Surprised, I responded: "Tell me more." This boy proceeded to tell me about a church near his school that had a fire that week and needed help rebuilding. He said that his school was working to help rebuild this church. As he talked, he slowly took from his pocket a small folded piece of paper. He unfolded it, slowly handed it to me, and said: "I was wondering if I could read this to the class and see if they want to help spread the light too?" I took the piece of paper and read the words written by this young boy:

> *Dear friends, next Sunday . . . I am making blueberry muffins to raise money for [a] church near my school. The walls of the church are falling in and they need help. With your help you can support my first grade class at [my school] to reach our goal of raising $1000 to help these children and families have a safer church to worship. Will you consider buying blueberry muffins next Sunday to help this cause? Thank you. Sincerely, [child's name].*

As I read these words a smile slowly formed as I made eye contact with this child. "I think this is a wonderful idea." During our time for sharing this young child stood up, hands shaking, and slowly unfolded his piece of paper and read his message. Following this time of sharing we moved into our time for offering. At this moment, another child spoke up: "I have an idea. We can save up all our offerings plus the [money from the sale of the] blueberry muffins and then we can donate it [all]."

Together the children discovered a way to help others as they shared the light in their local community. This story is one of many that I could share of children learning of God's love and then wanting to share that love with others. There are many others. Children respond to bullying and hate by offering support to their friends and by leading groups focused on inclusiveness and antiracism on their school campuses. Children respond to a global pandemic by making masks, decorating signs for healthcare workers, and painting kindness rocks to spread in their neighborhood when all are sheltering in place. Through this meaning-making process, children can discover language that helps them stick up for on another and stand for what is right, good, and just. We do children a disservice if or when we believe they are only in our presence to learn what we have to offer. Instead, part of the meaning-making process requires that we encourage and support them as they find ways to respond to all they are learning and experiencing by sharing it. Children want to do their part in helping spread the light so that Christ's light will be present in many places. It is in these moments that the light of Christ is shared and we have the awesome opportunity of witnessing the littlest child that leads us all.

When holy space is created for children to do this work, they begin discerning and identifying their call:

- "I experienced God when listening to my grandmother play on the organ . . . This made me feel really happy. I want to go to worship so I can hear my grandmother play again."
- "I experienced God while on the swing on my grandparents' farm . . . I like that feeling, I want to go back there again."
- "I give thanks for God's love. I want to share God's love with others. This week I'm going to be kind to my brother."
- "This week I shared God's light by asking a new student at school to sit with me at lunch."

The list of children's responses to God's presence is long and ever-growing. Each of their statements reminds me of the call to respond to all that we experience by paying attention and recognizing God's presence in our lives. Their reflection remind us that:

> Every single unit of existence . . . in the world begins with physical feelings and the most important of these feelings is the one from God. This feeling received from God is directive, offering a possibility of the occasion's best future.[20]

Children can discern their next steps towards this best future. Our work as adults is to encourage children in this process by asking: "I wonder what God is asking you to do next?" This is a question of discernment, call, purpose, and action. It's an invitation for them to return to this place of knowing and to begin this work again . . . to consider the possibilities and to choose how they want to respond. This is where we as adults can

---

20. Suchocki, *God, Christ, Church*, 39.

lead the children we are in ministry with to faithful action in their community and the world.

Journeying with children opens my eyes to all of the possibilities to respond to God's love as we share that love with others. It is a pure reflection of the greatest commandment to love God and to love neighbor. More importantly, this holy work is an essential part of their faith formation and their walk with God. With our guidance, encouragement, and support, children are eager and capable of doing this holy work. As children do this holy work, it is clear that they are the hands and feet of Christ. I'm privileged to journey with these young disciples through such moments and I stand in awe of all that they do to share God's love with others. Their praxis (faithful action) is a holy example for all in their community.

PUTTING THE PIECES TOGETHER

Engage, Recognize, Claim, and *Respond*: these are the four big pieces of the puzzle, the four big parts of a child's theological work, and the essential pieces of these children's meaning-making process. When we think about the kaleidoscope of life, the moving parts, the multiplicity of possibilities, the infinite patterns and creations, we see many colors and shapes moving continually through the spectrum of time. This four-piece process is how children make meaning out of all that life presents to them at any given moment on any given day.

As children *engage* in the Word and the traditions of the faith, *recognize* the presence of God and others, *claim* their own experiences, and *respond* to these experiences, they make meaning that informs and affects their individual faith narrative. Together, these four larger puzzle pieces provide a thick, rich description for the church as we affirm God's active presence in the lives of all persons, and journey with them as they participate in all that God is doing for the transformation of the world.

While at times this process feels rather rigid and linear, it's important to remember that children work through this process at their own pace and take twists and turns on the journey. The pieces do not have to go in any specific order; they move around as children experience the world around them. In doing the important work of engaging, recognizing, and claiming God's presence in their lives, children begin to hear God's call to respond, and they know what to do next. In responding to God's grace and love, they enter into another experience, another possibility, continuing their meaning making work in response to this new information and wisdom.

Using these four puzzle pieces, doing the holy work of meaning making, and participating in this theological process, children build their faith narrative and develop religious language to articulate and celebrate how God is working in their lives. Our work as the adults who journey alongside them is to encourage children in this process of reflection and faithful praxis. We do not need to concern ourselves with making sure they follow this process in a specific order. It is enough to invite children to wonder and to share. For in so doing, we create space for children to encounter God, recognizing that we do not so much bring children to God as create space for children to sit in the God's presence. We can support children in their theological work by modeling language and creating space for them to discover and practice their faith. Through our active wondering and listening, we encourage children in this work of engaging, recognizing, claiming, and responding to God's presence in their lives.

By doing that, our work becomes more about heart than head knowledge. Our work is not to pour information into our children, but instead to open a space for each child to discover their own understanding of God. The next chapter identifies tools that help us with this holy work.

chapter 5

TOOLS FOR THIS HOLY WORK

"We are going to help you with your work." —Anonymous (age 5)

As young theologians engage in the holy work of meaning making, they use various tools to help them in their theological process. My research identified a multitude of ways children engage and respond to God's presence in their lives. Consolidating these many learning approaches utilizing common themes and similarities, six tools emerged that help children do the important work of meaning making. These tools help children develop their own understanding about their relationship with the Divine. Recognizing that children learn about God in varying contexts and traditions, and acknowledging all children learn and process at different paces and in different ways, this chapter seeks to identify six tools that are helpful as they process their experiences and discoveries: Story, Liturgy and Ritual, Relational Awareness, Memory Markers (locations, objects, and symbols), Wonder, and Work. This chapter describes each of these tools that children use as they engage with God and one another in the faith community.

STORY

This tool showed up the most in the work of the children I have sat with. This comes as no surprise to me as a Christian who sees our faith tradition as one grounded and shaped by the stories God gives us in the Biblical text. In my work as a minister with children, I have told an endless number of stories to children, and in return those children have shared stories with me. Through this process of storytelling, it becomes clear how story invites children into a time and space where they can do the holy work of active wondering and meaning making. Story reveals the steps of the dance and when we are paying attention, story invites us into the movement. This ancient tool provides an entryway into imagination and discovery as children experience and find meaning in response to God's active presence in their lives.

As mentioned in previous chapters, one of my favorite stories to tell is the *Godly Play* story, *The Great Family*,[1] which is the telling of the Abraham and Sarah story found in the book of Genesis. Sarah and Abraham hear God's call and travel a long journey, moving from place to place. When I tell this story, I use manipulatives and move the characters across the desert (sand in a box known as the "Desert Box"). As the children watch the characters in the story of *The Great Family* move across the desert, they take note of the characters' names, the places the characters journey to, and the things that happen along the way. I have told this story numerous times, and as I write, one moment comes to mind: As I am telling the story, I see twelve children in a small room in a Chicago church lean in closer as their eyes widen and watch the pieces move from place to place. Their eyes stay focused on the desert box as the events unfold. As I near the end of the story, I say: "Abraham and Sarah had a son and they named him Isaac." As I say these words I show the children a wooden figure as one child excitedly says "What!?!" I continue the story, telling them how Isaac met and married Rebekkah, and as I say these words, this child watches and smiles. Then I say, "and then do you know what happened? They had children . . . and their children had children . . . and this went on for thousands and thousands and thousands of years." The child continues to lean in closer, watching more intently, and again, raises her eyebrows and silently mouthing "What!?!" again. It is then that I say: "This continued on until your grandparents had children and your parents had you! And so YOU are part of the great family." At this time, this young girl, who had started rocking back and forth on all fours, stops moving—she looks up at the desert box and slowly says: "Wow!" as she sits back on her heals, eyes never leaving the desert box. Silence follows until I break it with the question: "I wonder what your favorite part of the story was," and all of the children eagerly begin to respond. It takes a moment, and then I see this young girl raise her hand. I ask her again: "I wonder what was your favorite part of the story?" She responds: "When you told me I am a part of the great family."

Story provides an opportunity for us to learn and an opportunity to discover. As Dorothy Jean Furnish reminds us, the Bible is a living event.

---

1. Berryman, *Complete Guide to Godly Play*, 2:85–94.

Furnish's theory in "Rethinking Children's Ministry," affirms that children are born with a capacity for faith, they make meaning in response to their relationships and experiences, and through the process of reflection and response, they engage in the world through feeling.[2] Furnish offers a method that encourages all praxis to invite children to meet (encounter), feel (experience), and respond to the text.[3] According to Furnish, the Bible is an encountering event and all are invited into the story, experiencing the Holy, and growing in the faith. Elizabeth Caldwell in *I Wonder* echoes this sentiment reminding us how story, and in her case the Biblical story specifically, encourages the development of a faith language that then leads to an ability to articulate one's faith and theology in response to their experiences with the Bible.[4]

The importance of story becomes clear to me through the discussion that follows the telling of a story. Children are eager to ask questions and to respond to the events, the people, and the places. "I wonder when Jesus ate?" one child asks, as another child wonders: "What was it like to watch Jesus walk on water? That must have been SO exciting to see!" The importance of story also appears in the time spent wondering with children when I ask, "I wonder what your favorite part of today was." Often, their response is "the story," or they take time to share their favorite part of the story, "I liked it when the angel tells Sarah she is going to have a baby, and Sarah laughs." In my time with children, the moments when I most often see their focused attention, and when I can visibly see their facial and body reactions of intrigue, excitement, and wonder, come when the story is told. The story is "when we listen and talk about God," one child reminded me. "Indeed it is."

The stories we tell and the way we share the stories are both equally important. Biblical (Sacred) stories ground us in who we are as God's beloved children and help us begin to identify how God is inviting us to contribute to the living story—making a difference in the world around us. Secular stories that tell of people, locations, events, and challenges, all help us begin to identify with the pieces of the story as our worldview is broadened. The children in Chicago that I sat with were fascinated that I had lived in Texas, and vice versa. We can visit places that seem far away, learn about God's people in other situations, and receive wisdom from other cultures as our understandings deepen. Stories model for children

---

2. Furnish, "Rethinking Children's Ministry," 76.
3. Furnish, *Adventures with the Bible*, 35–37.
4. Caldwell, *I Wonder*, loc. 204–37.

ways to embrace and respond to varying emotions, and help them problem solve when a situation seems impossible. Favorites that come to mind include Dr. Seuss' *My Many Colored Days,* helping children identify their emotions and begin processing how to name and live in that space. *The Very Hungry Caterpillar,* helps us begin to understand creation as we experience how a caterpillar turns into a butterfly. What are some of your favorite stories to share with children?

How we tell stories is also important. Growing up, my favorite way to experience a story was when my Sunday School teacher would use a flannel board to move the characters around as they story unfolded. Now, as a *Godly Play* story teller, my favorite way to tell a story is with manipulatives that the children can see, feel, and work with. You might utilize a gifted story teller, actors, or the children themselves to share the story. You might listen to or watch the story. The options are endless, and nothing can replace sitting down with a book open, reading the story together.

Stories can be presented in numerous ways including a simple telling of the story, reading from a book, or acting out the story too. Remembering that all children learn differently we should always provide various ways for children to engage in different ways utilizing different learning styles and multiple intelligences learning theory. Manipulatives are especially helpful for visual and kinesthetic children. In my sessions I always include time for internal and external processing through times of silence and then an invitation to verbal discussion. I also make sure there is time for independent work as well as group interaction. Some children need more time to think and share then others and I try to honor that by carving space for thinking and speaking space in the time I spend with children. When a child who is eagerly raising their hand to participate and then after I call on them they exclaim: "I forgot," I respond by saying: "That's okay—would you like more time to think about your answer? I can call on you again in a few minutes . . ." Utilizing various mediums for response is helpful too. These might include but are not limited to: markers, paint, chalkboards, wipe-off boards, pipe cleaners, or retelling the story with the manipulatives provided. The key here is to remember, as a child in one of my groups boldly proclaimed, children learn differently. A classroom should affirm this by providing various ways to engage the children in the lesson and experience for that day.

Finally, the images and words we use also help to ensure every child is invited into the story and given an opportunity to consider: "Where am I in the story?" Several years ago, I was telling the parable of the good shepherd to a group of children. As described in Chapter 1, this *Godly Play* parable shares the story of the lost sheep in combination with the imagery of Psalm 23 and the image of God as the good shepherd. As I tell the story, I move different colored sheep through the events of the story. As the sheep explore and go wandering, one gets lost, and the good shepherd brings the lost sheep home. This particular day, when I asked the children: "I wonder what your favorite part of the story is?" A young boy eagerly responded: "When the good shepherd found the black sheep that looks like me!" And then when I asked: "I wonder where you are in the story," this young child exclaimed: "I'm the sheep that has been found!" In this moment I realized how different colored materials offer a diverse way for the children to engage and connect with the story. All too often, children's books and their illustrations do not present a diverse or multicultural representation of God's good creation. Here, this child's wondering and expression of his favorite part helped me see the importance of the materials and the illustrations used in stories. It is essential that they are diverse in their portrayal of all people, places, and things as a way to offer a variety of moments and images for which children will connect and make meaning.

Children enjoy being connected to, invited into, and incorporated in the unfolding of the story. They yearn for a space where they can actively participate and reflect on the information presented. When the story is told in an engaging way, children stop, and they pay attention. This does not mean that we have to entertain children or make the story flashy in order to get their attention, but it does mean we need to be intentional as we read and share stories with them. It is our work to invite them into the story, to wonder with them, and to encourage them as they engage with the people and events that take place. It is in this intentional space with this important tool that a space is created for them to begin making meaning out of what they see and hear.

LITURGY AND RITUAL

Children also experience God through liturgy and ritual. Liturgy, often described as the work of the people, consists of the words, actions, and rhythm that make up our time together. Ritual, a series of actions performed in a specific order, help shape our time together. Each of these tools appear in a child's meaning making process.

Holy Work with Children

In my ministry I have discovered that routine is essential. Sharing with the children the schedule or flow for the day invites them in as full participants, helps them know what to expect, and encourages them to discover their favorite part of our time together. This is extremely important in creating an inviting space for all persons to pay attention to how they experience God.

For centuries, Christian communities have relied on liturgy to help bring structure and order to their time together. Liturgy or "the work of the people," provides a community an intentional way to worship God together. In the midst of our busy world, structure and routine become even more important providing adults and children alike intentional moments to stop, to come together, and to connect to God and neighbor. Through liturgy we are invited into a familiar space as we engage in the holy work of worship.

How we order our time together matters. While different classes, services, groups, might order their time differently, it is important that we are intentional in structuring our time with children, creating a liturgical flow that teaches, models, and invites children to practice the actions of our faith communities. We need to make sure that there is a pattern and rhythm created so that all persons participating are able to feel the flow of the time allotted. This helps children know what to expect and gives them something to which to look forward to. Repeating liturgy and words weekly helps children to learn the words and gestures for themselves. When we follow a consistent flow or liturgy, children will learn what to expect and will begin to participate more fully.

When we do this work well children begin to experience each part of the liturgy as anchors, grounding them in the work and inviting them in as full participants. Each week children share their "favorite part" whether it is lighting the candles, adding to the offering plate, hearing the story, or praying. The list is endless and when there is an intentional liturgical flow each week children come back knowing that they will get to participate in their favorite actions again.

When I sit with children, they always remind me of the "order of the day." One child might tell me, "before we eat we need to pray." Another asks, "Are you going to start with your prayer singing?" Some remind me to light the candles, and others join me in saying the words we use to open our time together each week. We light the candles, and then they look up as I speak the familiar words: "The Lord be with you." In response, the children eagerly respond: "And also with you." We have conversation about how these are the words Christians in many communities use to greet each other and to remind each other that God is with us. When it comes time for prayers the children eagerly add to the conversation as they share their joys and concerns, and then join in chorus as we say the Lord's prayer together. Working through this order of events each week provides a consistency that helps young people thrive. They know what to expect, and over time they learn the words and are eager to participate and to add their voice to the conversation.

One week as I sat with sixteen children and we moved through our liturgy together arriving at the time for prayer, one child asked:

"Can I just tell you something that goes on in my family?"

I responded, "Of course!"

"At the end of all our prayers for our food, we say 'the only thing that's holding the world together is God when he's hugging us.'"

I responded, "That is a beautiful image, thank you for sharing. Would you like to say that at the end of our prayer today?"

The young boy nodded yes and so we all prayed, concluding our prayers with: "and God is holding us together with a hug, Amen."

This is one example of how liturgy can shift and change with input from the children. As children participate they bring their own opinions and wisdom to the process. Following this conversation, this young boy's theological statement became part of our weekly prayers—it became an essential part of our liturgy and time together. If ever the young boy thought that we might forget, at the end of our prayer he would say—don't forget my part! And then he would boldly lead the group in this concluding statement.

When I concluded my research, I wanted to find a way to share all that I had learned with the children who journeyed with me over those seven weeks. As I thought about how to affirm the wisdom they had shared with me, the image of puzzle pieces came to mind. "They are helping me put the puzzle together," I thought. And so, I created a puzzle with multiple pieces that represented the individual pieces of wisdom each child shared with me. When I finished this story, I sat back and asked the anticipated question: "I wonder what your favorite part of the story was?" One child eagerly responded—"when you said that we help put the pieces together!" Adding their thoughts, prayers, and voices to the liturgy, the children demonstrated how they were invited, welcomed, and included in this community. Through liturgy (words, actions, and order) the children entered in, joined, and shaped this community until it became their own. Each child added to the dance—the steps we took as we journeyed with God and each other, growing in our understanding of and faith in our creator.

RELATIONAL AWARENESS

The third tool shown to me by children is their relational awareness of God, self, and others. This reflects the research findings presented by David Hay and Rebecca Nye. In their conversations with children, Hay and Nye discovered that children have a consciousness, or awareness, of "I-Others, I-Self . . . I-World . . . and I-God."[5] According to Hay and Nye, this relational awareness adds "value to their ordinary or everyday value . . . [it] lies at the rudimentary core of children's spirituality, out of which can arise meaningful aesthetic experience, religious experience, personal and traditional responses to mystery and begin, and mystical and moral insight."[6] Relationships are one tool that help children make meaning of their experiences as they connect to God.

Children have a relational awareness that helps them make meaning out of their experiences. As children begin to do the work of understanding self, others, and God they begin to take in information and make meaning from their experiences, giving them insight on which to build their narrative and their faith story.[7] Through their actions, wondering, and work, it became clear that the children are very aware of themselves, of each other, and of God.

---

5. Hay and Nye, *Spirit of the Child*, 109.
6. Hay and Nye, *Spirit of the Child*, 109.
7. My research affirms three of Nye's dimensions for relational consciousness: I-Self, I-Others, and I-God. The dimension missing in my findings is the I-World awareness. This is not a critique of Nye and therefore is not an attempt to negate Nye's work around the I-World dimension. Instead it is a statement of reflection and transparency. For an unknown reason the children I worked with for my research did not specifically reveal their awareness of the world outside of their relationships with themselves, their community, and God. Perhaps the research questions/methodology did not lend itself to this display of awareness. Another theory is that this is one space where we can grow as educators, helping children increase their awareness of the world that is larger than their everyday experiences.

Self

Children express a sense of their awareness of themselves as they talk about their discoveries using "I" language, reflecting on their own experiences. Children share their own preferences, "I like," their own thoughts, "I wonder," and their own feelings, "I was scared when." Sometimes their answers resemble the answers of other children. Other times children's answers are unique as they clarify and explain giving specific reasons for their opinions. "I like spring and summer. I like summer the best—because it's my birthday." Children also share stories that seem important to them, and experiences that continue to have meaning for them. One third grader shared when reflecting on the story of the lost sheep: "I have been lost. I went on a field trip when I was in first grade at the aquarium. I got lost. It was scary." Another child shared her own experiences: "I like swinging on the swing at my grandparents farm, it makes me feel close to God." Awareness of self also shows up in children's work as they respond to the story through art and play. Children often know exactly what they want to work with, and when they are unsure they are able to take time to consider the options and then make a decision. "I like to build, I think I'll work with LEGO bricks." "Today I want to draw, the paints look fun. While some children need time to reflect, to consider options, and to share their thoughts, when we create space and time for children to do the work of reflection they show their ability to narrate their thoughts, experiences, feelings, and desires. It is a tendency of educators and adults to rush through reflection, providing answers to children, or sharing our own opinions. When we jump in too quickly, we run the risk of disrupting the child's ability to access their self-awareness and prevent them from finding the words to express what they are thinking, feeling, or experiencing. It is essential that we find ways to create space and time for children to do the deep thinking necessary for this work, and then to listen attentively as they find words to express their thoughts.

God

Throughout this book thus far I point to the many ways children talk about, relate to, and experience God. This points to their deep awareness of God and their relationship with the Divine.

The first time I gather with children, I often tell the *Story of the Light*, as described in Chapter 2.[8] When I tell this story, I light a big white candle in the middle of the circle and then as I tell the story, I use the flame from the big candle to light individual tea lights for each child. As I light the tea candle, I look at the child, call the child by name and say: "This is your light." Following this story, I ask: "I wonder how you experienced God in this story?" Responses vary as children share how they see God in the story: "I saw God in the story because he was the big white candle and we were all the little candles." As children reflect together, their wonderings often build on the previous responses, as they offer their own reflections and wonderings. Often children engage in a theological conversation as they reflect on their understanding of God: "God is good." "God shares his light with us." "God's work is helping people." For these children God is very much in relationship with humanity.

Another story I often tell is *The Crosses*.[9] In this story, I show the children different crosses and share a brief history of each cross design. Following the story, as the response segment of our class time began, one child went off to work with the crosses as his instrument of choice. I watched him as he began to set up all of the crosses in a circle on his tray. After working for a few moments, he stopped and exclaimed: "Look—when they're all in a circle I think they all form God." I went to the area where he was working and asked him to "tell me more." This young person paused and then continued his reflections: "God is in each of us [pause] God is with all of us, [pause] God connects us to each other."

This child's theological reflection highlighted the relational nature of children, and demonstrated this child's awareness of his connection to God and to others. As educators we sometimes focus on teaching information to children, instead of creating space for children to reflect on their own wonderings. When we fail to create space for children to reflect and share, we miss a huge opportunity in helping them grow in their theological understanding and relationship with God. One of the questions I continually ask children is: "I wonder how you experienced God this week?" This question draws awareness to our relationship with God and invites children to pay attention.

As children practice asking and answering this question, their confidence grows as they seek to discover God in all aspects of their life. When

---

8. Stewart and Berryman, *Young Children and Worship*, 71–76.
9. Berryman, *Complete Guide to Godly Play*, 4:69–73.

I first began my research in Chicago, I boldly asked this question at the end of one of my sessions. I handed out disposable cameras to children and asked them to take pictures as they experience God during the week. At first they looked at me in silence and I thought "well I guess we'll see how this goes." As time went on and we spent more time together, I intentionally asked this question everytime we gathered. At the beginning of a session I ask: "I wonder how you experienced God this week," and then at the end of the session I encouraged them to "Pay attention this week and come back and tell me how you experienced God." As the weeks passed the children returned with excitement to share their experiences. One child said: "I can't wait for you to develop my pictures—I took SO many . . . God is everywhere!" The excitement continued to bubble and the children's desire to share grew so much that one day I met a young child from my group at the grocery store and he ran up to me exclaiming: "Pastor Tanya! Can I tell you now how I experienced God this week?" It was a joyful moment as we stopped in the midst of the ordinary to share and celebrate God in our lives.

The more we tell stories and create space for children to share theirs, the greater the possibility children will begin to hear and see God at work in their lives. Children have a relational awareness that helps them do this theological work. Our work as educators is to make sure there is space, and interest for children to share and reflect on these experiences. The child's relational awareness of God and others allows them to recognize how different narratives provide information into how God is moving in their lives. Whether the text is ancient or new, written or oral, sharing our experiences and hearing the experiences of others provides opportunities to learn and grow. It is in these moments that children capture God at work in their lives giving them important information as they continue to make meaning and develop a deep understanding of and relationship with God.

Others

The third and final dimension of relational awareness presented by the children's work and wonderings is their relational awareness of themselves and others. Names are especially important to children. Whenever I meet with a group for the first time, there is always great conversation around what my name is and what they are supposed to call me. I also make sure there is time for me to hear the children's names too—focusing on what they like to be called and how to pronounce their name correctly. Each time I tell the story of the light, I become even more aware of the importance of names. One specific day, after I told the story of the light, a child chose to work with the story during the response time. Since this story involves fire, I worked alongside him. As he worked to remember and retell the story, I asked him a few questions: "Do you remember who these lights are for? Who are we lighting them for today?" This child proceeded to pick up each individual candle, state another child's name, and after we lit the candle together, carefully set it down. He went through the entire list of the children in the class that day, and then he said: "But there are others who are not here today—I think we should light their candles too!" After all the class candles were lit, this child asked: "Do we have extra candles?" "We do," I replied. "Can I have a few more? I'd like to light a candle for my mom, and for my friends, and for other kids who I do not know yet." After naming and lighting several more, this child sat back on his knees, reflected on his work, took a deep breath, and then said: "Now there is just one more." "Who's light is this?" I asked. "Mine," he replied. At the end of the response time I asked: "I wonder, how does working with the story help you experience God?" He replied: "It helps me remember that God's love is everywhere and can touch everybody."

Through their actions, wonderings, and work children show their awareness of other people. They recognize and name their family, friends, people in their communities, and sometimes people they have never met. Relational does not apply "in a narrow sense either. Its reference [is] not limited to family, friends, or foes."[10] "I know this girl—she had an accident in the gym—so I need to pray for her." "In each case the child's awareness of being in relationship with something or someone was demonstrated by what they said and, crucially, this was a special sense that added value to their ordinary or everyday perspective."[11]

One of my favorite activities is to put up a large wall-sized world map. I then invite children (and adults) to add their prayer requests using sticky notes, placing the note near the location where the prayers are needed. It is always amazing to see the prayers the children lift up, placing their post it notes all over the map as they pray for people in their home, local community, and the world. Focusing on the other people who journey alongside them helps expand the child's awareness of their greater community.

10. Hay and Nye, *Spirit of the Child*, 110.
11. Hay and Nye, *Spirit of the Child*, 110.

Providing them opportunities to name their friends, family, and community; to offer prayers for those close to them and those they do not know. As Nye argues it is through these relationships that children make meaning. "In this 'relational consciousness' seems to lie the rudimentary core of children's spirituality, out of which can arise meaningful aesthetic experience, religious experience, personal and traditional responses to mystery and being, and mystical and moral insight."[12]

Children's relational awareness of others highlights the importance of community in their meaning-making process. As children engage in this process, their relational awareness provides a tool that equips them to recognize how the words in liturgy and story connect to them as individuals, as God's beloved creation, and as part of the faith community. The story and liturgy do not simply reflect something that happened at a specific place or time to some unknown character. Instead, the child's relational awareness of God and others allows them to recognize how the text provides information into how God is moving in their lives. This realization creates a space for children to make deep connections and meanings in response to the text presented because the story says something about them, about God, and about others.

Relational Awareness and the Meaning-Making Process

As children begin to do the work of understanding God, self, and others, they begin to take in information and make meaning from their experiences, giving them insight on which to build their narrative and their faith story. Through this process, the children's relational awareness provides a way for them to identify and name the moments when they experience God. As they recognize God's presence, they utilize their relationships with God, themselves, and others as they describe and claim their experiences. Through their relational awareness, children recognize their place within God's creation and hear how the story provides information about themselves, about others they care about, and about God.

Spirituality, as asserted by Nye, is something children already have. Children's relational consciousness therefore becomes a tool that equips children for recognizing the Holy's presence in their lives and in the lives of others. This relational awareness offers children a lens to see and experience the world as they recognize how they are in relationship with others and with

12. Hay and Nye, *Spirit of the Child*, 110.

God, making meaning as they learn to trust and engage in these relationships. It is through this lens that children begin to make meaning from their experiences, recognizing God's presence in their lives. Relational Awareness helps children identify their place in God's holy dance.

MEMORY MARKERS: LOCATIONS, OBJECTS, AND SYMBOLS

The fourth category of tools that children use to make meaning as they connect to God and others are memory markers. Memory markers are children's ways of remembering what they have experienced and learned as they do the holy work of making meaning.

Early in my research experience I told the story of *The Great Family*, described in Chapter 3. When I tell the children this story, I identify all the places Abraham visits and stops on his journey. I also note the moments when he takes a break to pray and give thanks to God. In the *Godly Play* story, when Abraham stops to talk to God, the storyteller builds an altar out of small stones to mark where Abraham had these holy conversations. One day as the children and I wondered about the story together I asked, "I wonder what your favorite part of the story is?" One child responded eagerly: "I liked Abraham's stampers." "Stampers?" I asked. "You know," the young girl responded pointing to the small piles of stones laid out before her, "the places where Abraham stopped to pray . . . he stamped where he talked to God." "Aaaahhh I said, I get it." For this young child stampers became the terminology she used to mark where a character met God. This day I responded with a new question: "I wonder what the stampers are in your life?" She immediately responded "In the sanctuary where I talk to God when I pray." Another child responded: "In my car when I tell my mom about my day." What followed was an amazing conversation as the children shared all of their holy moments, identifying the stampers in their lives that help them remember and share their experiences with God.

Over time I came to identify these "stampers" as "memory markers," because as I listened to the children it became clear that this is what they were doing—they were marking their memories. As they shared their stories they were very clear as to where they were, what they were doing, and if there was something that stood out to them in their holy moments. "I experience God when I'm at my *grandparent's farm*, sitting on the *swing*, and looking out at the *pasture*." As I listened to children's stories over the years that would follow, I began to notice how most often every narrative includes a location, symbol, or object that sticks out in the child's memory. I began to learn that not only are these tools children use to remember their stories, but they are also tools those journeying with children can use to help children document and claim their experiences so that they will remember and can return to those moments and discoveries time, and time, again. I imagine if I ever see the little girl who describes her grandparents farm so beautifully again that I will ask her: "Tell me again about how you experienced God at your *grandparent's farm,* when you were sitting on the *swing,* and looking out at the *pasture."* My hope is that she will not only remember but that we could then have a conversation about what she learned about God that day and perhaps what she learned about herself and the world around her.

The children's use of memory markers (locations, objects, and symbols) in their meaning-making process reveals tools the children use to claim their experiences. These tools become the memory makers, the stakes in the ground, the bread crumbs that help children remember where they have been. As both Piaget and Vygotsky assert, these are the symbols and images that help children make meaning out of their experiences. According to Piaget, the use of symbols and images reflect one way children begin to think concretely, to develop connections between what they are seeing and feeling, and eventually to develop the ability to reason. Making these connections provides children with tools to begin thinking abstractly, expanding their understanding of the world around them. The candle, in the story of the light, might at first represent a physical light (or candle) seen and held by the children during the telling of the story. Over time, the big candle became "God's light" leading to the realization: "God is one light and without God there wouldn't be any light." Through the identification of locations, objects, and symbols, children's new realizations will ultimately impact how they make meaning of the faith narrative and their own faith story. Location is important because it gives children a tangible memory, a visual image of a specific time and place. By reflecting on the location of an event, children are able to revert back to that moment providing a space for them to remember and claim the meaning made and the wisdom gained from their experiences. Symbols and objects provide a tangible item that they might either carry with them or see in different times and places, serving as a continual reminder of when they experienced God. Fowler asserts that it is through the use of symbols that children begin to engage in speech and play. These become tools for the children to use as they tell and retell their experiences of God.

In the midst of the COVID-19 global pandemic, I often wonder: "How are our children experiencing this new reality? What meaning are they making?" During this pandemic by son has become fascinated with masks. When I put on my mask he immediately reaches for it as if to ask: "What is this? Why are you wearing it?" I always do my best to explain, modeling language as I try to help him make meaning in response to current events. I wonder if the masks his parents and caregivers wear will continue to be a "stamper," a reminder of this specific time in his life. I wonder what associations he will have as his body recalls these moments. Will he remember the anxiety and stress felt during this time? Or will he recall what it feels to be loved? During this time, my son's school invited children to paint "kindness" rocks that they could then disperse throughout their neighborhoods to bring joy and hope to all who might see them. My son, only fourteen months old eagerly picked up a few of the kindness rocks and then helped me, as he rode in his wagon around our neighborhood, place them strategically in our neighbors' yards. Upon running into a neighbor we said: "We just put a kindness rock in your yard. We hope this makes you smile and brings you joy during this difficult time." She smiled and said: "Thank you! This means a lot—that you would think of me." When we got home, I made sure to place one in our yard that I plan to save as a memory marker of this time for my family. While, our son might remember this time when he sees pictures of us all wearing masks, I can also pull out the kindness rock and say: "It was a difficult time. It was a hard time. And—here is a rock, a stamper, that helps us remember how we shared God's love and joy during this time too."

Our children are internally aware of all the complexities of life. Our work is not to shield them from the brokenness but instead we are called to help them process and verbalize their wonderings, their concerns, and their learnings. It is through this meaning-making process that we can encourage them in the work of recognizing and claiming God's presence and love in the midst of it all.

Locations, objects, and symbols therefore, represent memory markers or place holders, helping the children remember the specific events of their stories. These markers reflect essential pieces of children's narratives and their meaning-making process. Children use these tools to claim their experiences as they make meaning that will become an essential part of their faith narrative on which they will continue to build and rely. The meaning made in these memories, as captured and claimed via locations, objects, and symbols, become the building blocks for children as they continue to grow in their awareness of God and deepen their faith.

WONDER

In Chapter 3 we discussed how adults can use active wondering to create space for authentic and honest conversation. This is an important pedagogical tool. It is also the fifth spiritual tool that children use to engage, recognize, and claim God's presence.

Creating a place for children to wonder and use their imagination is essential to their meaning-making process. Wondering offers children an opportunity to make meaning as they enter and respond to the mystery of God. Through wondering children take time to process internally or externally what they are experiencing and begin to sort through that data as they initiate the meaning-making process that deepens their understanding and strengthens their faith. As children reflect on and respond to their experiences, they begin to make connections and their synapses fire as they create "memories" storing the information for future use. This becomes the foundation on which children build their faith narrative storing experiences, ah-ha moments, positive (or negative) memories, and any insight gained along the way. These connections become the essential pieces of the child's narrative as they develop, grow, and learn.

Wondering begins with the understanding that there may be more than one answer to a given question. The children's active wondering gives them a way to imagine and wonder out loud and in community. It gives them an opportunity to learn and to each. To share observations and to make meaning with others. The open-ended question of "I wonder" helps children recognize that all answers have value and that when we share and engage in dialogue with one another we learn and grow. "A wondering model invites children to have a conversation with the Biblical story . . . to hear or read the story with question marks, not periods . . . [while] inviting children into the story in ways that will make them want to return to it again."[13]

My faith has been deeply impacted by the deep wondering I have experienced with individuals younger and older than myself. As mentioned in Chapter 3, it is hard work to create a space where individuals of all ages feel

13. Caldwell, *I Wonder*, loc. 939–68.

safe enough to wonder out loud without the fear of being judged, corrected, or shamed. It takes time to create a safe space. My experience has taught me that taking this time is essential and the results are invaluable. Every time we open a conversation, participants pick up on something they may not have noticed before. As that young child stated: "I wonder is a good word."

As children wonder, they discover and practice using the Christian language, they work to make sense of their surroundings, they grow in their understanding of the world, and they identify how God is calling them to respond. We can wonder with children as they share their thoughts and feelings. As children get older story provides an opportunity for their imaginations to consider different viewpoints and experiences giving them a depth of knowledge and wisdom on which to build their own understanding, personality, and identity. Again, Chapter 3 provides some guidance on how to do this important work.

In the time I have spent in ministry with children, they continue to teach me the importance of questions. In my final reflections with the children I worked with during my research project one child stated: "You ask a lot of questions." And another one responded: "And you listen when we talk." Through this faithful and attentive dialogue, we learned together. During one session, a young child shared: "I have a question . . . What if you are at school and you experience God and you don't have anyone to talk to about it?" I responded: "That is a really good question, I wonder what you all think?" The discussion that followed led to the children problem solving together, discussing several options including writing it down, talking to God, and talking to their mom or dad after school. This is one example of many similar conversations I have experienced. I continue to find that when I create the space, ask the question, and believe in the children's capacity to respond, the children show up more faithfully and authentically than I could ever imagine. Through these conversations they learn more about themselves, more about each other, and more about the God who created and loves them. They also discover ways to hear God's voice and to do God's work too.

WORK

Wonder engages children in the process of reflecting on their experiences and leads them into a time of discernment as they consider how God is calling them to respond. It is through this process that a child identifies their work and begins seeking ways to respond with faithful action.

Just as the young child in Chapter 4 identified a way to help the church who lost their building to a fire, other young people discover ways they can respond to God's presence and love too. As one child reflected on her experience in worship: "I experience God when my grandmother plays the organ in church. This is why I'm learning how to play the piano so I can make music for others to enjoy during worship too." Through my *Godly Play* training I began to see how a child's work is play. This is the process where knowing and being come together helping a child discern their meaning and purpose in life. Through play, a child does the important work of recognizing, claiming, and responding to God's presence in their lives.

Just like an adult's work looks different from one person to the next, a child's work can look different too. Some play and learn through outdoor or physical activities such as a nature hike, or a game of soccer with friends. Others learn by building with LEGO bricks or silently working with art supplies like paint or crayons. Just like adults, a child's gifts and interest typically shape their work and I have also discovered that children are much more open to trying new things and other possibilities too. Therefore, work and the time for response should be left open, providing space for children to use their imaginations and to play as they find new ways to highlight and share all they are experiencing.

Following the liturgy of worship and of the *Godly Play* curriculum, my time with children moves from story to wondering to a time for work or response. This is when children are invited to choose an activity from the shelves to help them process and respond to the story that day. I try to keep the activity shelves stocked with an array of options. Some children choose to work with the story, using the manipulatives to retell and process the story of that day or a story they heard prior to that session. Others choose LEGO bricks, crayons, paints, or chalk. A favorite of the children who joined me for my research project was the black wipe off board that lit up making their artwork glow. No matter the form of play the children are invited into a space where they can work independently as they process the story and listen to God. An example of this that I see in my ministry is when a child will be present for baptism or communion during a worship service, and following that service they will go home and play "Baptism" or "Communion." Parents will call me ecstatic exclaiming: "You'll never guess what my child did today! They went to their room after we got home, and when I checked in on them they were baptizing their dolls!" or "They came into the kitchen and asked me for some bread and juice because they wanted to play communion!" I always listen while smiling as I am never surprised but delighted by these stories. When children are given space to play, they are given an opportunity to process and make meaning out of all they have experienced. This is true for church experiences too. Unfortunately in today's busy world full of structured activities there is less time for unstructured and independent play where children can really work out all of their feelings and learnings in response to their experiences.

Sometimes a child's work leads them to identifying a small step they can take to change the world around them: "I am going to go home and share God's love by cleaning my room," or "God is asking me to listen to my mom." Other times a child's work leads them to bigger discoveries and ideas for making a greater impact on the world around them. "I am going to go to my school and see if we can start a recycling program," or "I wonder if my friends can all send letters to our state representative sharing our feelings about this?" If you search the internet for "Children making a difference" you will find over one billion hits sharing the numerous ways children are making a difference and changing the world around them. The children I have journeyed with are some of the most empathetic and creative people I know. When given space to do the work of moving through the meaning-making process, they engage in both knowing and being, and they discover what God is calling them to do and they identify how they want to respond.

As ministry leaders, our job is to create space for both independent and communal unstructured play. We can provide children with choices and guide them as they choose their work, and then we have to step back and let them do their important work. It is important to give children permission to choose their work based on their individual interests and skills. In individual class settings we might invite children to read (the Bible or other stories about God), to be creative with art supplies, to work with a labyrinth, to act out the story with props, or to journal. We can invite them to go outside as they engage in their time of work, or we might create space for play in our classrooms. In the church, we can invite and encourage them to participate in the faith community. They can help lead worship as acolytes, greeters, ushers, readers, and even preachers! They can be on ministry teams, sharing their ideas as churches discern how to lead one another in stewardship, outreach, or other ministries. They can participate in age appropriate ministry opportunities too such as helping serve a meal to the poor, making artwork to send to shut-ins, or collecting supplies for people in need. The possibilities are endless. The important step is that churches pay attention to the young people in their communities and give them real and valuable opportunities to play and to work using the gifts God gives them.

Children, just like adults, are called and equipped for the holy work of making a difference in their communities and in the world. As they move through their meaning-making process, they engage, recognize, claim, and respond to God's presence and love. Thankfully God gifts them and us with the tools we all need to do this holy work. Together we discover new ways to deepen our faith, strengthening our relationship with God and neighbor. This is the work God calls all of us to do, no matter our age. As ministry leaders it is our work to create space that invites children to play and to do holy work as they process and discern ways God is calling them to respond to all they are learning and experiencing.

LOOKING AT THE KALEIDOSCOPE

As we continue to think about the kaleidoscope of life, we recognize how this metaphor reflects the multiple pieces and the numerous possibilities created in the image one sees through the plastic lens of the toy. The process of becoming and God's transformative work in and through creation reflects an ever-changing kaleidoscope of possibilities, meanings, and discoveries. As children participate in this dance, life's kaleidoscope of possibilities, they do so, just like all other persons, through the lens of the meaning-making process. As the children engage, recognize, claim, and respond to God's presence in their lives they take in and make meaning from their diverse array of experiences. This process invites them to participate in all that God is doing in and through creation as the children are guided through their wonder, play, and discovery.

The tools children use to participate in this process: Story, Liturgy and Ritual, Relational Awareness, Memory Markers (locations, objects, and symbols), Wonder, and Work, help them do the important work of making meaning. It is with these tools and through this process that children make meaning out of God's active, relational, and effective presence in their lives.

chapter 6

FAITHFUL PRAXIS

Partnering with God's Children

> "We really are all in this together." —Anonymous (age 10)

PARTICIPATING IN THE DANCE TOGETHER

Children are theologians. They participate in a meaning-making process as they recognize, claim, and respond to God's presence and love. This is God's transformative dance. As shepherds, we support and guide children in this dance. This is the faithful praxis that God calls us to as we join in ministry with children. The word praxis comes from the Greek word, πρᾶξις, translated roughly as a deed, function, or action. Just as children have taught me that our experiences of God lead to a faithful response, our call and desire to journey with children leads to faithful action where we commit to doing the holy work of journeying with children as they grow in love of God and neighbor. We recognize and claim God's presence in the lives of the young people in our communities and we respond with respect, intentionality, and care. Our faithful praxis includes the work to create safe space and to engage in holy conversations as we practice active listening and wondering with children in our communities. Through our actions we can create a nurturing space for children where they can participate as full members in the faith community.

By journeying alongside children, we make a difference in each other's lives, in our communities, and in the world. Together, we grow in love of God and neighbor. Together, we share that love with others. Together, we transform the world to reflect God's beatific vision. As one of the children with whom I worked stated so eloquently, "We really are all in this together."

Our Calling

As I reflect on the conversation I share in the opening of Chapter 1, I see that young child clearly as he looked up at me and I hear his parents say: "He has a question for you." I can still see the hesitancy in the child's eyes as he asked me his theological question: "How do I know I believe in God?" This was his invitation for me to join him in holy conversation. I could have brushed him off. I could have offered him a short and simple answer. Or I could have gotten down on eye level, taken a deep breath, and prayerfully tried to find a way to respond to his invitation with respect, grace, and intentionality. I like to think that I chose a messy version of number three—accepting the invitation and responding with respect and care. This is an example of faithful praxis.

This young child was calling me, an adult, to show up, to listen, to wonder, and to be honest. He was inviting me into a theological conversation. I am so very grateful that I did not let the busyness of that Sunday morning rush me away from this child and that conversation. I am so very grateful that I allowed my breath to slow me down and opened my eyes and heart to this young child and his wonderings. I am so very grateful that this child conversed with me. For that conversation changed me. It prompted me to attend to God's calling—not only to listen but to learn and to grow.

I have returned to this conversation many times over the last thirteen years. I don't know what in particular prompted his question that day, what made it so urgent to him that he would get his parents to bring him to an unfamiliar church and track down a pastor. I can only imagine that he was wondering whether an adult would take him seriously. Prompted by that child, I have grown to value the space and the work in which we participated together that morning. In those short minutes, this young child revealed an awareness of God and a deep desire to engage in theological reflection. I feel fortunate to have been invited into that conversation. I am grateful that we had an opportunity to wonder together. Together we both stepped out in faith. We listened to and affirmed one another. Together we reflected on and discovered God in our midst. This is the faithful praxis God is calling us too.

Our Work

Children reveal an enormous amount of wisdom for religious educators, the church, and the world. It is to this wisdom that I now turn to consider how we can engage in faithful praxis that invites, listens, nurtures, and guides children as they participate in their meaning-making process, a process in which they use and develop tools and practices that will help them throughout their lifelong faith journey.

My goal in ministry as practical theologian is to make space to listen to and learn from children. In this space we partner with children in the meaning-making process and God moves and transforms us all. My prayer is that leaders in ministry with children will pay attention to this work with intentionality and care, so that when a young child asks us: "How do I know I believe in God?" we will respond with respect, curiosity, and love. This is our work. This is the faithful praxis God is calling us too. We must shepherd the children in our midst as they seek to make meaning in response to their experiences with God and others.

This work begins with the call to show up, listen, wonder, and offer our own honest reflections too. Through this process we can create safe space, nurture relationships, and invite conversation that helps people of all ages strengthen their relationships with God and neighbors. Our work is to partner with children, as we learn about God and discover faithful ways of living together. Together we participate in what God is doing for the transformation of the world.

PUTTING THE PUZZLE TOGETHER: CREATING A HOLY KALEIDOSCOPE

Working with children reveals the process through which children move as they engage, recognize, claim, and respond to God's presence in their lives. These are the pieces of the meaning-making puzzle, the parts to the whole, the movements to the dance. These pieces look different to every child. They take shape and form in different times and places too. As children go through this process, this dance of meaning making, they develop and use spiritual tools that help them recognize and respond to all that God is doing in their lives. Specifically, it is the tools of Story, Liturgy and Ritual, Relational Awareness, Memory Markers (locations, objects, and symbols), Wonder, and Work, that I have found helpful in shaping and forming their dance of meaning making, or, for the young boy with whom I began this book and this chapter, the dance of becoming aware of God's presence in their lives and the world and responding to it.

If you have ever looked through a kaleidoscope, you have seen the beautiful images a multiple-pieced collection of glass or plastic fragments can make. The mirrors and colored fragments together make a beautiful pattern of color and light. Yet when the person twists the kaleidoscope, the unique pattern instantly changes—forever. The same can be said of every individual's meaning-making process. We join in God's transformative dance bringing our color, light, wonderings, and learnings. Sometimes we move to our own rhythm, and other times we come alongside and move with others. It is a beautiful thing to witness, but if we are not paying attention, we miss the beauty of what God is creating with us. Moments come and go, wonderings surface and fade away, discoveries emerge and shape the next moments in time. This holy dance that we co-create with God is beautiful and awe inspiring and merits our attention.

To dance with her offers the child respect, love, and grace. It also affirms that every person shows up in their own beautiful and unique way. As one child reminded me, "I liked how you affirm that we all learn differently and experience God in different times and places . . . sometimes our teachers forget that."

Children will not necessarily leave a one-hour Sunday school class with all the answers. Nor will they leave with a solid faith that will never be questioned, changed, or discarded. But by joining children in this process of engaging, recognizing, claiming, and responding to God's active presence in their lives, the children (and the adults who journey with them) will begin to discover their own meaning and understanding in response to God's presence (both in their lives and in the lives of others). Through such awareness, they begin to claim God's presence and love as they wonder: "How is God calling me to respond?" "What difference can I make?"

Children move in and out of the pieces of this process in different ways at different times. It's not a linear process. When we create space, show up open to all the possibilities, and provide guidance and encouragement, then we can trust God and the child to do the rest of the theological work.

Holy Work with Children

FAITHFUL PRAXIS

In the final pages of this book, we revisit the concepts introduced in previous chapters and begin to imagine what faith formation with children might look like if we pay attention to how children make meaning and respond to God's presence in their lives.

Today's World

I am writing this chapter in the midst of the COVID-19 pandemic. Never before have ministry and faith formation needed to be as fluid and flexible as now. Now ministry with children happens at church, at home, online, and in every life moment in between. Wherever and whenever that might be, the church's task is to invite children and families to do the important work to which God is calling them.

Particularly in a time of physical distancing and sheltering in place, connection and reliable relationships are essential. This includes peer relationships and intergenerational relationships. Children need shepherds and guides who not only model the faith but come alongside to practice and learn together.

Families are overwhelmed and exhausted. Some might pick up a curriculum to try around the dinner table at home, but others are still trying to find their table. Still others are gathering in their car, on a hike, at bedtime, in a park, with a computer or a book.

No matter our circumstances, whether in a time of pandemic or war, of hurricane or fire, when we pay attention we can connect to God and each other every moment of every day. Such connection can be brief or protracted, can happen in nature or cooped up in our homes. It depends only on our availability and attentiveness.

Our Work

During the pandemic, one of my favorite daily moments is at bedtime when my husband and I sit down with our son, who is now fifteen months old, and we read a story, and then someone asks: "What are you grateful for?" followed by "What are your prayer concerns?" In these moments my family slows down and takes time to connect to God and each other. We've created space for active listening and wondering. We built a ritual of a bedtime story, a liturgy of reflective questions, a family prayer, and the Lord's prayer. We honor relational awareness as we give thanks for each other, for friends and family, and for our community and world. This also provides time to wonder together, to mark our memories, and to recall both our favorite moments and our hard moments of the day.

As I think about this ritual and liturgy that my husband, son, and I have created together, I now see space for adding a wondering question that leads to response: "I wonder what God is calling us to do tomorrow?" I am excited to see how God uses this time as my family and I continue to practice together as time passes and our son grows and changes too.

As ministry leaders we can create such space, such ritual, such liturgy, and such opportunity to make meaning for the children and the families with whom we are in ministry. But it means being ready and staying connected to God and to those about whom we care. It means getting our bodies ready to do this important work, be that through stillness, music, journaling, prayer, or physical activity. When we are ready, we will feel focused and energized, open to all of the possibilities that God presents in and through our ministry with children.

Once we are ready, we can engage in the work to which God has called us. The rest of this chapter helps you get ready. It puts together everything we have discussed thus far and maps out a strategic plan for developing a faithful ministry with children.

Getting Ready

We begin our work by creating a safe space for children and their families to come and participate in the holy work of meaning making. In this safe and welcoming space, children will hear that their experiences, stories, and thoughts matter. Through active listening and wondering, they will see the process of meaning making modeled and be invited to practice and participate in this important work. Children and adults will be affirmed and nurtured as they wonder what their stories say about God, others, the world, and most importantly they will learn to ask and recognize how they show up in the story.

I often describe this process as "setting the table well." I grew up in a household where if the table was set there must be something exciting happening. Bonus if it was the dining room table and the china/crystal! This is true in many faith traditions too. In the Christian tradition, the act of setting the table for communion is done with care and purpose. This should be true also of the space we are creating for ministry with children. For in-person ministry, we do this work by physically getting the space ready—by making sure there is a space for children to gather, that supplies are readily available, and that everything is located at a child's level. For digital synchronous ministry, we create this space by using tools that ensure digital safety and interactive tools that encourage children's participation. For digital asynchronous learning and at home faith formation, we create this space with content and experiences that make it easy for children and their families to participate together.

The Invitation

As a child I loved receiving mail. I would eagerly go down the street each day and would carefully peek into the mailbox as I anticipated what might be waiting. Maybe it was a postcard documenting my grandmother's travels, or could it be an invitation to a party? One day when I was about seven years old I discovered a note from one of my Sunday School teachers. I must have missed Sunday School the week before because in the note was a message that stated that she missed seeing me, that she was praying for me, and she looked forward to seeing me again soon—would I be back this week? My heart soared as I thought: "Wow! She noticed!" I ran home and said: "Mom! We have to go back to church this week. My teacher invited me!"

More than thirty years later I am sure children still love to receive mail, and more importantly they yearn to be seen and hope to be invited. Once we do the work of setting the table well, our next step is to invite. If we simply wait, we may be disappointed by the empty chairs that remain. An intentional invitation to the table and into the meaning-making process is essential.

One Sunday, as I was wrapping up my time with my Sunday School group, I wondered aloud: "I wonder how you will experience God this week?" As I blessed them on the way out the door, I said: "I look forward to hearing how you experience God the next time we are together." A few days later, I was on the train when I saw one of my children. He quickly ran up to me and said: "Pastor Tanya, I experienced God this week at the beach," and he excitedly told me how he recognized God in that encounter. This moment made me realize that this child was not only excited about the question but was ready and excited to share with me. My invitation to wonder and share opened space to pay attention and to share his experiences. Imagine what would happen if we continuously offered an invitation and created space for children to share their God moments with us?

Our invitations will undoubtedly vary. We can send an invitation like my teacher did many years ago, we can make a phone call, when we are sitting with children we can make a simple invitation, like "Come and sit with me," or a ask a wondering question inviting them to share their experiences of God.

Invitations come through verbal and visual cues. We can invite persons in or make them feel excluded by our body language, by the way we behave, or by the way a space is set up. If children walk into a room where everything is taller than them, or if non-readers walk into a room in which everything is labeled, they will sense that they are not welcome. Visual cues matter as much as spoken ones.

Manipulatives, physical objects and pictures also invite participants into the process of meaning making. In my research, I realized early on that children loved being part of candle lighting, so that became part of our ritual. Recall the story of the light, and how children watch candles being lit, one for each child present. The children's fascination with the lighting of the candles brought them into the story that I then told. Participating in the liturgy, they began to make meaning in response to what they were seeing and hearing. The physical lighting of the candles, and the repetitive words spoken, provided the children with an opportunity to reflect on what it means for every person to have a light. Talking about lighting a candle and actually physically lighting the candle present two very different ways of inviting children to engage in the meaning-making process.

Whether online or in person, faith formation with children requires that we set the table well and that we offer an invitation to the table too. Our invitation to children opens a space for them to explore all of the possibilities, to engage in the work of meaning making together, and to discover God's presence and discern our response to God and the world. When we are intentional, when we plan ahead, and when we set our hearts to this work, children will feel our welcome, hospitality, and care, and they will look forward to joining us in this important work.

HOLY WORK WITH CHILDREN

PARTICIPATING IN THE MEANING-MAKING PROCESS

Engage

Once the safe space is created and the invitation is sent, children and adults gather and begin to engage with God and one another. One of my favorite moments in my time with children is welcoming them into our classroom. If I am seated on the floor, I invite them to sit on the carpet with me and the other children. As we begin to form a circle, I use this time to talk to the children about their week. "I wonder how you experienced God this week?" I might ask. Or, "I wonder what your favorite part of this week was?" Another favorite: "Is there anything you want to share with us as we wait for your friends to arrive?" I then move into a time of getting ready where I say: "It is time to get our bodies ready to listen to the story. I like to get ready by singing, will you sing with me?" Following the song I take a deep breath and sometimes invite them to take deep breaths with me, or we might say a breath prayer together. One of my favorites is: "Breath in and say God be with me. Now breath out as you say help me listen to you." Then I say: "I think we're ready, let's begin." I slowly take out the manipulatives for the day's story, and I slowly and intentionally begin to tell the story. Through this process all are invited in and we begin to engage in the meaning-making process together.

Children are more likely to engage when their leader is fully present and engaged too. When we show up as a non-anxious presence, calm, and prepared, children are more likely to participate. For this reason, I begin my work with children with intentional time to get my body ready. I arrive early, I make sure I have all the supplies that I need and then I sit in my space in the circle and pray before a child ever enters the room. This time of preparation is essential and ensures that I and others can begin well. I begin by remembering the call and purpose of my ministry, and I ask God to help me guide the children so that they will grow in their love of God and neighbor. I also ask God to keep me open to learning and growing too. When we commit to this work with intentionality and purpose, we create a space that honors children and the work God calls them too. In this space children open up and begin to engage with God and others. This is the beginning of their holy work.

As the children and I move through the day's liturgy together we experience the different pieces in their structured order: Gathering, Story, Response, Feast, Offering, Prayers, Sending Forth with blessing. As discussed

FAITHFUL PRAXIS

in Chapter 5, liturgy and ritual alongside story are the tools for keeping children engaged in the meaning-making process. These tools provide a structure to our time together and help everyone relax into the flow of the day knowing what to expect. While there are always surprises as we experience God together, we are assured by the pattern and the flow the liturgy creates inviting us into the story and the meaning-making process.

Recognize

As children engage with God's word through story and liturgy, we can invite and encourage them to pay attention by asking: "I wonder how you experienced God in this story?" "I wonder how you experienced God today?" These questions are invitations to strengthen relational awareness (Chapter 5) as children recognize God at work in the child's life, their community, and in the world too. Listed below are questions and examples to help you in this work.

Awareness of God

- I wonder how you experience God in this space.
- I wonder how you experienced God today.
- I wonder when you felt close to God this week.
- I wonder when God felt far away.
- I wonder what reminds you of God's presence and love.

When I practice recognizing God with children, I take time to ask the question, give them space to share their answers, and then find a way to affirm and bless their experience. For example, when I take my son outside I might say, I wonder what reminds you of God. If he points to a tree then I'll say: "That is a tree. It is part of God's good creation. Thank you God for trees." In this way, I recognize God in our interaction, and my son hears my awareness of God.

Awareness of Self

- I wonder what you are good at.

- I wonder what your favorite color is.
- I wonder what you like to do in your free time.
- I wonder what is hard for you.

We help children develop an awareness of self by calling them by name and showing interest in who they are and what they like—and remembering! One of my favorite times of year is creating and preparing for children led worship, the moments when children create and lead worship for our faith community. In preparing I always ask children to prayerfully consider how they would like to participate. I am always amazed to hear back when they say: "I really like to read, so I want to read scripture." Or "I really like to pray—can I do that?" I also learn when they say: "I do not like to be in front of people, so is there something else I can do?" I'm always amazed at what they share about themselves when I give them space to discern and share. When we ask children questions about themselves, we provide an opportunity for them to reflect and to share. This encourages the development of their awareness of self as they recognize their own interests, gifts, and role in the world around them.

Awareness of Others

- I wonder who helped you this week.
- I wonder who showed you God's love today.
- I wonder who made you feel sad or angry.
- I wonder who your friends are.
- I wonder who you will share God's love with today.

"I wonder who" has become one of my favorite wondering questions to help children recognize God at work in their relationships with others. One Sunday I asked a young child, "I wonder who shared God's love with you this week." She excitedly responded, "My best friend! I was having a really hard day, and my friend gave me her cookie at lunch and told me she hoped it would make me feel better. I think God's love is like that!" This young child and I then had a conversation about how the actions of others can help us see and feel God's presence and love. If I had never asked the question this might have remained a nice gesture that brought this young girl joy. An important experience, and this conversation provided space to reflect on the experience allowing it to deepen our understandings of how others impact us and show us God. When we invite children to consider how they are impacted by others, we help them grow in their awareness of others, and we help them recognize God at work in their relationships with other people.

Awareness of World

- I wonder what cities/states/countries you have visited.
- If you could travel anywhere in the world, I wonder where you would go.
- I wonder if there is anywhere in the world that needs our prayers today.
- I wonder what part of God's creation you would like to know more about.

We expand a child's awareness of the world by helping them see beyond their present reality. We do not have to get on an airplane to learn about communities, countries, people who are different than us. There are ways to help children do this work without leaving their current location. In one of my ministry settings, I created stations for children to work at. One of the stations was the world experience where children could read headlines or articles and learn about the world. They were then invited to offer prayers for the world either by journaling, putting a prayer on a post it note and then placing it on the wall map of the world or by placing a confidential prayer in the prayer box. Expanding a child's worldview opens up more diverse possibilities for them to recognize God at work. "God is at work here, there, and everywhere!" A young child exclaimed. "Indeed God is," I replied. "Thank you God for taking care of all people in all times and all places. Amen"

We nurture relational awareness with the questions we ask, the stories we tell, and the language we use. This is an essential part of the faith formation process. When ministry leaders participate in holy conversation with children we have an opportunity to model relational awareness and then to invite children to develop it too. Relational awareness then helps children recognize how God is at work in and through all of creation. This awareness and recognition then leads them into the work of claiming and responding to God's presence too.

Claim

As children engage and recognize God in their lives, they begin to claim a deeper understanding of how God is actively present in their lives. When invited and encouraged to share, children use the memory markers described in Chapter 5 to tell their stories and to share their experiences. These memory markers help children keep track of where they had been, what they have done, who they were with, and what they experienced. When we ask children to share their experiences we create space for them to mark their memories through storytelling as they claim their experiences and make meaning out of them. Questions that help children with this work include:

- I wonder how you experienced God this week.
- I wonder what you were doing when you experienced God this week.
- I wonder who you were with.
- I wonder what it looked/smelled/felt like.
- I wonder what you want to remember most about this experience.
- I wonder how we can remember together.

It is especially important that the leader follow up to the question repeating what they heard and then as appropriate asking another question. For example: "I hear that you experienced God at your grandparents farm . . . I wonder what you were doing?" Sometimes we might have to sit and wait in silence too as children get used to us asking questions and take the time they need to process their thoughts and discern their response. For this reason it is essential that leaders in ministry with children learn how to create space, ask questions, and sit in silence as we model and practice story sharing with the children in our community. Providing time for all persons in the room to engage in open conversation is essential. This is how we model and practice this process together.

My experience has taught me that maintaining a safe space encourages listening and discourages judgment. By asking open ended questions, and avoiding leading questions, I find children are more willing to share. "I wonder what you think" vs. "I wonder what the answer is." "I wonder what your favorite color is" vs. "Do you like yellow?" We create space for children to share their stories and claim God's presence when we wonder without expectation or judgment. As children share their experiences, my responses tend to be simple: a slight nod of the head or a quiet "thanks for sharing." Other times I might repeat what they said back to them, "Hmmm . . . You experienced God when your dad gave your mom flowers because the flowers remind you of love." Sometimes, if I did not understand completely, I would ask a follow-up question, "I wonder how the flowers your dad gave your mom remind you of God?" The child's response (as she looked at me directly): "Love." It is in these moments when the memory markers (location, objects, symbols) are stated and affirmed that children's brains engage in the important work of creating memories. Their synapses fire making new connections in their brain helping move their experience from short term memory to long term memory as the child attempts to hold on to this important experience. This is how they claim their experiences with God.

Offering different ways to process their experiences is helpful as children claim their experiences too: journaling, drawing, placing pictures in a photo box or album are just a few of the possibilities. Following the telling of the Good Shepherd story, I watched a young child create a scene with LEGO bricks. As the end of our "work" time ended, I approached him and asked if he would like to share his work with me. He eagerly said, "yes" and then explained that he had created a tractor for a farmer to ride through the fields and then he exclaimed: "God shows him which way to go—just like the good Shepherd!" I thanked him for sharing just as he added: "God shows me the way too!" In these moments of creativity, wondering, and sharing children find ways to claim their own faith understandings and narratives.

Milestone celebrations are another way we can mark and help a child claim an experience. One of my favorite milestones to celebrate every year is the blessing of backpacks. This is a time when the faith community offers a prayer and blessing for all students and educators. Every time I lead this ritual, I try to include a memory marker—in the beginning it was a small ribbon tied on the backpack as I was saying the blessing and now it has grown into a backpack tag with a scripture or words of the blessing on it. The idea is that this memory marker will serve as a visual reminder to the child/educator so that when they are in their various places of learning/teaching they can see the memory marker on their backpack and remember "I am loved." "God is with me." This memory marker helps individuals claim their narrative: God is with me. I am loved. I am not alone. Etc. While I try not to get too focused on giving away stuff—trinkets or extra plastic items that end up in a box somewhere—I do try to help children identify memory markers that help them claim and remember meaningful experiences.

Helping children claim their experiences increases the possibility that these memories might continue to shape and form them as they grow. The meaning that they make as they claim their experiences and understandings will continue to support them now and in the future as they lean into God's presence especially in moments of loneliness, grief, or uncertainty. As children claim God's active presence in their lives, this awareness of God's presence becomes part of their narrative and hopefully their identity.

Respond

As children work through their meaning-making process and as they claim their own theological understandings, they show me how their discoveries lead to a response. As one child shared: "God showed me the way, now I can help others."

As identified in Chapter 5, the tools of wonder and work help children with this piece of the process. When I create space for children to wonder and for them to process all they are learning through individual and group work, I am amazed at the discoveries and insights they share. As we have journeyed together, I have learned to follow up their wonderings and work with one final question: "I wonder what God is calling us to do next?"

Recall the young child who baked and sold muffins with the intent of raising money for a local church that experienced a fire. In the space created for wonder and work, he discovered a way to respond. This shy, quiet, and withdrawn child trusted the space enough and found the courage to ask me and the other children to support him in this effort. In response to his suggestion, another child asked if their group's weekly offering money could go to help the church too. When children feel safe wondering out loud they can begin imagining, dreaming, and creating. When they are encouraged in their work they discover all sorts of amazing ways to respond to the world around them.

Children continue to tell and show me that they learn differently. As educators we encourage children to wonder and to engage in work by providing opportunities, various mediums, and space for free play and reflection. It is important to note that this is not necessarily handing every child the same color sheet after reading a bible story, but instead providing multiple options, stations, possibilities, where children can choose how they want to respond, they can work without restrictions, and they are encouraged to engage the process with their creativity and imagination. When I have the privilege of journeying with children—this time devoted to work is often my favorite as I witness children finding ways to respond to the day's story and to God's presence in their own unique way.

One of my favorite memories of my time with children is looking across a room and seeing several children working and responding in their own way. One child is deep in reflection as he moves his fingers through a sand labyrinth. A young girl sits with colors as she draws the candles of the community, quietly mouthing the name of the other children in the room as she points to each candle that she created on her paper. A third child sits in the middle of the space building with LEGO bricks. He is the one who would later share—"God shows me the way too!" It is a beautifully diverse picture of what response can and should look like—and we as leaders in ministry with children get to experience and participate in it! It is a tremendous honor and a gift to be part of this deep and holy work.

"What are you going to do next?" I often ask. "I'm going home to help my mom cook lunch." "I am going to tell my baby brother I love him." "I am going to bake cookies for my neighbor." They hear a call to pray for their friends, to share with their neighbor, to feed the hungry, or to participate in a church's ministry that is striving to share Christ's light with others. While seemingly simple these next steps create a path for children to move from claiming God in their life to the important work of responding to God in their lives.

PARTNERING WITH CHILDREN

As I look back on my twenty plus years of ministry with children and recall the memories from this four-month research project specifically, I find myself smiling and tearing up as I see the children, remember their names, and wonder: "Where are they now?" My hope and prayer is that they have continued to be guided by faithful shepherds encouraging them as they make meaning and respond to God's grace and love. I also hope that they are doing the important work of shepherding others too.

I am grateful to every young person who has shown me how they participate in God's divine dance. As full participants in God's transformative work they move through the kaleidoscope of life as they find ways to love God and neighbor. Children approach this work with eyes and ears, hearts and minds, wide open. Through a multiplicity of experiences children do the holy work of making meaning and responding to God's grace and love. Engage, Recognize, Claim, and Respond: These are the puzzle pieces that children pick up, turn around, consider, and practice as they dance with their beloved creator. These pieces do not flow in a specific order but instead mimic the spontaneity of each child's movement.

As children participate in the divine dance, they carry and use the tools in their toolbox, Story, Liturgy and Ritual, Relational Awareness, Memory Markers (locations, objects, and symbols), Wonder, and Work. These tools help them as they discover the meaning of God's presence and love. When tools are not used, they become dull and rusty, and individuals begin to feel disconnected from God and others. Therefore, it is important that children are encouraged to sharpen and practice using these tools so that they remain accessible on the faith formation journey.

As leaders called to ministry with children, we are invited into this dance, partnering with and shepherding these young theologians. It is a privilege and an honor to come alongside the youngest members of our communities as we do this important work together. When we commit to an intentional ministry that partners with children, we can create a holy space for them to do the important work of meaning making.

The church has an important role in this work too. As an intergenerational community, we participate in the dance together. We pay attention, listen, and affirm each other honoring God's presence, grace, and love that dances within every person and all of life's experiences. The kaleidoscope of life offers unending possibilities and views of how God is actively at work in and through the world. Sometimes we just need someone else to help us see it. For this reason, faithful ministry with children must establish a community where all persons can imagine and wonder together.

Our work begins with a deep respect for and understanding of the meaning-making process. We remember that every person develops and grows in response to their experiences, and their reactions to those experiences. Faithful praxis must create a space that acknowledges, respects, and nurtures the process of meaning making while helping the children develop, sharpen, and practice with their tools. Therefore, as we develop our ministries with children we must ask:

- How are we joining children in the process of making meaning?
- How are we helping them engage, recognize, claim, and respond to God's presence in their lives?
- How are we helping them develop the tools (story, liturgy, relational awareness, memory markers, wonder and work) that can help them in this meaning-making process?

As we ponder our answers to these questions, we are invited into a creative process as we claim our role in the divine dance. The options are many as we seek to create a space where children engage, recognize, claim, and respond to God's presence in their lives. The possibilities are endless as the kaleidoscope of life continues to shift creating a space for religious education that seeks to help children make meaning out of their experiences. We begin with the question: "How do I know I believe in God?" and an open and curious posture and approach: "Maybe we can learn together . . ."

appendix

RESEARCH METHODOLOGY

Wondering with and Listening to the Children

> "I wonder is a good word." —Anonymous (age 8)

I am a practical theologian seeking meaning and transformation in the everyday lives of individuals and the church. Affirming God's presence in the lives of children, I minister using active listening and qualitative research. In this project, I looked deep into the child's reality, seeking to understand how children experience and make meaning in response to God's active presence in their lives. Together we thought about the future of the church.

Two questions guided my research:

1. How does listening and paying attention to the experiences of children affirm God's active presence in the lives of all persons, challenging conventional theological anthropology, particularly in regard to children?

2. How do these stories reveal insight for religious education in the church and the world as children and the entire faith community journey together, recognizing, claiming, and responding to this Divine presence, working together for the transformation of the world?

RESEARCH METHODOLOGY, METHODS, AND EPISTEMOLOGY

Using qualitative research methods, I placed myself as an observer actively listening to and then attempting to interpret the meanings the children expressed. My specific project used grounded theory, participant observation, and active listening built on Jerome Berryman's *Godly Play* curriculum and liturgy.

Before engaging the project, I sought review and approval of the Human Subjects Research Committee (HSRC) at Garrett-Evangelical Theological Seminary. This process required me, the researcher, to be completely transparent, reveal the exact plan for the project, provide the exact questions that will be asked during the process, and develop permission forms where children, their families and their churches could agree to participate.

I sought to create a space where children and their families felt invited in and connected to the process. Ethical dimensions of research were primary for me. Aware of the issues regarding power, authority, the interrelationship of race, gender, social class, level of education, and ability, I faithfully attended to "work together to provide equity, safety, and parity."[1] Together we built a community of learning discovering God's presence in the world as I listened to their needs and provided an opportunity for them to hear my initial findings and to offer feedback in response to my discoveries.

RESEARCH DESIGN AND CONTEXT

Set-up and Design

Children need a safe place that acknowledges and affirms God's grace in their lives.[2] Therefore, the first task in this study was to recognize the inherent value of the children's experiences. As an adult analyzing children's stories, it is possible to assume and to misinterpret the insights the children share. I carefully set up the space, choosing supplies, and creating the liturgy in a way that welcomed children's full participation. I observed, collected data, and confirmed my conclusions with them.[3]

Communities

I worked with two different locations: Site 1 (a diverse urban church via a Sunday morning session) and Site 2 (a multicultural neighborhood

---

1 McIntyre, *Participatory Action Research*, 13.
2. Swinton and Mowat, *Practical Theology and Qualitative Research*, 11.
3. Denzin and Lincoln, *Sage Handbook of Qualitative Research*, 24.

Appendix: Research Methodology

church via an after-school session). Prior to the beginning of the research sessions, I worked as the Director of Children's Ministry at Site 1 and as a volunteer at Site 2 to build relationships. Throughout all the work, I intentionally followed each site's child/youth safety policy. This included needing another trained adult in the room with me at all times. For this reason, I recruited and trained two Research Assistants (one for each site) who helped me supervise and lead each session as well as contributed to the work of data collection too.

In order to create safe space, I was transparent holding informational meetings for the parents and guardians of the children. I also met with the children as well, sharing the process with them, inviting them to consider participating, and then soliciting the consent from both parent/guardian and child.

Data Collection and Analysis

I recorded all verbal and visual communication with my computer and an external microphone. In addition, I used an iPhone to record data and to take pictures of the children's work. Finally, using the video recording feature I recorded individual conversations with children. In these ways, I was able to capture multiple dialogues happening during each session.

Secondly, I collected the children's artwork each week for analysis. At the end of the research project, I took pictures of their work for my records and returned the work to each child. Many of them also provided me with their cameras (given to them at the beginning of the project), sharing the discoveries that they made during the week. These pictures added essential information to my data collection.

Finally, my own journaling and self-reflection became an essential way for me to document the events of each session, my feelings in response to each of them. With all of this work, I have an extensive documentation of my process, the decisions I made, and my responses to each session.

Data Analysis

Following the completion of the first five sessions, I took a month to transcribe and code the data collected at each separate site. The transcription process became an intentional time where I listened and watched each session, documenting each child's verbal and nonverbal responses to each

Appendix: Research Methodology

piece of the liturgy and each wondering question. I also went through the data which had been collected on my iPhone, adding pictures taken (including pictures of the children's artwork), and any verbal conversations recorded. Where applicable, I also added any notes from my journal, the RA's feedback, and iPhone recordings. After the transcriptions were complete, I began work to code and organize the data.

Then, I created a rich description to present back to the children as their story during our final session together. I reminded them that they were helping me with my school project, and that each week their wonderings and discoveries provided another piece to the puzzle. I used puzzle pieces and images to describe the different categories I discovered to the children. I showed them each piece, explaining the picture (and thereby the category), telling them what I had learned. As I shared a piece, I set it down and added it to the final puzzle. When the puzzle was complete, I told the children that they had taught me a lot, and through our time together they had shared Christ's light with me.

Following this last session with the children, I returned to the data once again, transcribing the final sessions and reflecting on the complete data. I finished my work by comparing and analyzing the sites together. I took the codes that emerged at each site and analyzed them, looking for similarities and differences. What emerged were my discoveries and findings that provide the wisdom for this book.

CONCLUSION

Through this process, a new method for working and doing research with children emerged. Active wondering became the most beneficial process for my work as researcher. Engaging in these open conversations created a safe space for us to wonder together, revealing the children's thoughts and discoveries.

We learned together as we wrestled with the mystery of faith together. This method opens space for children to share their voice, develops critical thinking skills (in response to the modeling done by the researcher and the work done by the children practicing this process), and helps all participants not only recognize but reflect on God's presence in their lives as they wonder, learn, share, and teach each other. As one child said, "Wonder is a good word." Indeed it is.

BIBLIOGRAPHY

Andrade, Alison. "Using Fowler's Faith Development Theory in Student Affairs Practice." *College Student Affairs Leadership* 1 (2014) Grand Valley State University. https://scholarworks.gvsu.edu/cgi/viewcontent.cgi?article=1014&context=csal.

Baker-Fletcher, Karen. *Dancing with God: The Trinity from a Womanist Perspective*. Atlanta: Chalice, 2007.

Berryman, Jerome. *Children and the Theologians: Clearing the Way for Grace*. New York: Morehouse, 2009.

———. *The Complete Guide to Godly Play: Volume 1*. New York: Morehouse, 2007.

———. *The Complete Guide to Godly Play: Volume 2*. New York: Morehouse, 2017.

———. *The Complete Guide to Godly Play: Volume 3*. New York: Morehouse, 2006.

———. *The Complete Guide to Godly Play: Volume 4*. New York: Morehouse, 2003.

———. *Godly Play: An Imaginative Approach to Religious Education*. Minneapolis: Augsburg, 1991.

———. "Silence Is Stranger than it Used to Be: Teaching Silence and the Future of Humankind." *Religious Education* 94 (1999) 256–72.

———. *The Spiritual Guidance of Children*. New York: Morehouse, 2013.

Bowlby, John. *Attachment*. 2nd ed. New York: Basic, 1982.

———. *Attachment and Loss, Vol. III: Loss. Sadness and Depression*. New York: Basic, 1980.

———. *Child Care and the Growth of Love*. Baltimore: Penguin, 1965.

———. *A Secure Base: Parent-Child Attachment and Healthy Human Development*. New York: Basic, 1988.

Boys, Mary C. *Educating in Faith*. Lima: Academic Renewal, 1989.

Bruner, Jerome. "Celebrating Divergence: Piaget and Vygotsky." *Human Development* 40 (1997) 63–73.

Bushnell, Horace. *Christian Nurture*. Eugene, OR: Wipf & Stock, 2000.

Buttrick, George Arthur. *The Interpreter's Bible, Vol. 7: New Testament Articles, Matthew, Mark*. Nashville: Abingdon, 1951.

Caldwell, Elizabeth. *I Wonder: Engaging a Child's Curiosity about the Bible*. Nashville: Abingdon, 2016.

———. *Wondering about the Bible with Children: Engaging a Child's Curiosity about the Bible*. Nashville: Abingdon, 2020.

Bibliography

Cobb, John B., and David Ray Griffin. *Process Theology: An Introductory Exposition.* Philadelphia: Westminster, 1976.
Coles, Robert. *The Spiritual Life of Children.* Boston: Houghton Mifflin, 1990.
Couture, Pamela D. *Seeing Children, Seeing God: A Practical Theology of Children and Poverty.* Nashville: Abingdon, 2000.
Crain, Margaret Ann. "Redefining the Fundamental Questions." *Religious Education* 101 (2006) 438–42.
Crain, Margaret Ann, and Jack Seymour. *Yearning for God: Reflections of Faithful Lives.* Nashville: Upper Room, 2003.
Denzin, Norma K., and Yvonna S. Lincoln, eds. *The Sage Handbook of Qualitative Research.* Newbury Park, CA: Sage, 2011.
Erikson, Erik. *Identity and the Life Cycle.* New York: Norton, 1980.
Fin, Gary Alan, and Kent L. Sandstrom. *Knowing Children: Participant Observation with Minors.* Qualitative Research and Methods 15. Newbury Park, CA: Sage, 1988.
Fowler, James W. *Faithful Change: The Personal and Public Challenges of Postmodern Life.* Nashville: Abingdon, 1996.
———. *Stages of Faith: The Psychology of Human Development and the Quest for Meaning.* San Francisco: Harper, 1981.
Fox, Nathan, and Greta G. Fein, eds. *Infant Day Care: The Current Debate.* Norwood: Ablex, 1990.
Furnish, Dorothy Jean. *Adventures with the Bible: A Sourcebook for Teachers of Children.* Nashville: Abingdon, 1995.
———. *Experiencing the Bible with Children.* Nashville: Abingdon, 1990.
———. *Exploring the Bible with Children.* Nashville: Abingdon, 1975.
———. "Rethinking Children's Ministry." In *Rethinking Christian Education: Explorations in Theory and Practice*, edited by David S. Schuller, 73–84. Missouri: Chalice, 1993.
Gilligan, Carol. *In a Different Voice: Psychological Theory and Women's Development.* Cambridge: Harvard University Press, 1993.
Goldingay, John. *Volume 1: Psalms 1–41.* Baker Commentary on the Old Testament: Wisdom and Psalms. Grand Rapids: Baker Academic, 2006.
———. *Volume 3: Psalms 90–150.* Baker Commentary on the Old Testament: Wisdom and Psalms. Grand Rapids: Baker Academic, 2008.
Griffin, David Ray. *God, Power, and Evil: A Process Theodicy.* Philadelphia: Westminster, 1976.
Hartshorne, Charles, and Creighton Peden. *Whitehead's View of Reality.* New York: Pilgrim, 1981.
Hay, David, with Rebecca Nye. *The Spirit of the Child.* Rev. ed. Philadelphia: Kingsley, 2006.
Heller, David. *The Children's God.* Chicago: University of Chicago Press, 1986.
Jensen, David H. *Graced Vulnerability: A Theology of Childhood.* Cleveland: Pilgrim, 2005.
Keely, Barbara Anne, ed. *Faith of Our Foremothers: Women Changing Religious Education.* Louisville: Westminster John Knox, 1997.
Kraus, Hans-Joachim. *Psalms 60–150.* Minneapolis: Augsburg, 1989.
Kris, Deborah Farmer. "What's Mentionable Is Manageable: Why Parents Should Help Children Name Their Fears." https://www.washingtonpost.com/news/parenting/wp/2018/09/20/whats-mentionable-is-manageable-why-parents-should-help-kids-name-their-fears/.

Bibliography

LaCugna, Catherine Mowry. *God for Us: The Trinity and Christian Life.* Chicago: Harper One, 1973.

Mays, James Luther, ed. *Psalms, Interpretation: A Bible Commentary for Teaching and Preaching.* Louisville: John Knox, 1989.

McFague, Sallie. *Life Abundant: Rethinking Theology and Economy for a Planet in Peril.* Minneapolis: Augsburg, 2001.

McGregor, Wynn. *The Way of the Child: Helping Children Experience God.* Nashville: Upper Room, 2006.

McIntyre, Alice. *Participatory Action Research.* Thousand Oaks, CA: Sage, 2007.

Mercer, Joyce. *Welcoming Children: A Practical Theology of Childhood.* St. Louis: Challis, 2005.

Miller-McLemore, Bonnie. *Let the Children Come: Reimagining Childhood.* San Francisco: Jossey-Bass, 2003.

Moltmann, Jürgen. *The Coming of God: Christian Eschatology.* Minneapolis: Fortress, 2004.

———. *In the End—the Beginning.* Minneapolis: Fortress, 2004.

Neville, Morgan, dir. *Won't You Be My Neighbor?* Focus Features, 2018.

Newman, Barbara M., and Philip R. Newman. *Theories of Human Development.* New York: Psychology, 2007.

Nye, Rebecca. *Children's Spirituality: What It Is and Why It Matters.* London: Church House, 2009.

Oxford Languages. "Recognize." https://www.google.com/search?q=recognize&rlz=1C5CHFA_enUS701US701&oq=recognize&aqs=chrome..69i57j69i59l3j0l2.1915j1j7&sourceid=chrome&ie=UTF-8.

Patton, Michael Quinn, ed. *Qualitative Research and Evaluation Methods.* Thousand Oaks, CA: Sage, 2002.

Piaget, Jean. *The Child and Reality: Problems of Genetic Psychology.* New York: Grossman, 1972.

———. *The Construction of Reality in the Child.* New York: Basic, 1954.

Piaget, Jean, and Barbel Inhelder. *The Psychology of the Child.* New York: Basic, 2000.

Poling, James N. *Listening for God: Toward a Constructive Practical Theology.* Minneapolis: Fortress, 2011.

Poling, James N., and Donald E. Miller. *Foundations for a Practical Theology of Ministry.* Nashville: Abingdon, 1985.

Rahner, Karl. "Ideas for a Theology of Childhood." In *Theological Investigations: Further Theology of the Spiritual Life* 8, 33–50. New York: Herder and Herder, 1971.

Robinson, Edward. *The Language of Mystery.* London: SCM, 1987.

———. *The Original Vision: A Study of the Religious Experience of Childhood.* New York: Seabury, 1977.

Rogoff, Barbara. *Apprenticeship in Thinking.* New York: Oxford University Press, 1990.

———. *The Cultural Nature of Human Development.* New York: Oxford University Press, 2003.

Seymour, Jack. *Mapping Christian Education: Approaches to Congregational Learning.* Nashville: Abingdon, 1997.

Sharapan, Hedda. "What We Can Continue To Learn From Fred Rogers." https://www.fredrogerscenter.org/wp-content/uploads/2016/10/October-2016.pdf.

Stewart, Sonja, and Jerome Berryman. *Young Children and Worship.* Louisville: Westminster, 1989.

Bibliography

Suchocki, Marjorie Hewitt. *God, Christ, Church: A Practical Guide to Process Theology.* New York: Crossroad, 1989.

Swinton, John, and Harriet Mowat. *Practical Theology and Qualitative Research.* London: SCM, 2006.

The United Methodist Church. *The Book of Discipline of the United Methodist Church.* Nashville: United Methodist, 2012.

———. *The Book of Worship of the United Methodist Church.* Nashville: United Methodist, 1992.

Vygotsky, L. S. *Mind in Society: The Development of Higher Psychological Processes.* Cambridge: Harvard University Press, 1978.

———. *Thought and Language.* Cambridge: MIT Press, 1988.

Whitehead, Alfred North. *Process and Reality: Corrected Edition.* New York: Free, 1978.

Yust, Karen, et al., eds. *Nurturing Child and Adolescent Spirituality: Perspectives from the World's Religious Traditions.* New York: Rowman & Littlefield, 2006.

www.ingramcontent.com/pod-product-compliance
Lightning Source LLC
Chambersburg PA
CBHW071453160426
43195CB00013B/2090